THE RIGHT WAY TO MAKE JAMS

In the same series

Handbook of Herbs

Uniform with this book

THE RIGHT WAY TO MAKE JAMS

Cyril Grange F.R.H.S.

RIGHT WAY

Typeset in 11/12pt Times by County Typesetters, Margate, Kent.

Printed and bound in Great Britain by Cox & Wyman Ltd., Reading, Berkshire.

The *Right Way* series and the *Paperfronts* series are both published by Elliot Right Way Books, Brighton Road, Lower Kingswood, Tadworth, Surrey, KT20 6TD, U.K.

With many thanks to
Margaret Hanford
for all her help.

CONTENTS

INTRODUCTION

Our ancestors successfully made, by rule of thumb, vast quantities of jams and preserves to save money, provide winter food and preserve home-grown garden and wild produce.

Scientific research gave us valuable practical information which ensured safe storage, provided superior products, and avoided failures.

In recent years an awakened desire to make jams from home-grown, pick-your-own or cheaply-bought produce has become apparent, mainly because of the high and increasing cost of commercial jams and, in some instances, the poor quality.

The making of jams at home is simple, successful, economical and money-saving. It provides a delicious food which is health-giving, energy-making, nutritious, appetite-boosting, and useful for many culinary purposes as a sweetmeat, on bread and butter or on toast, in sandwiches, scones, and for puddings, pies, cakes and many other purposes such as fillings, sauces, icing – there is no end.

Equally valuable are the money-saving preserves of jellies, conserves, butters, cheeses, marmalades, curds, pickles, chutneys and ketchups.

The recipes given here are formulated from much research and experimentation in the author's kitchen; from recipes of proved value from skilled housewives over many years and from scientific investigation by research stations at home and abroad.

When this book was originally written, imperial measurements were used. In this revised edition, the approximate metric equivalents have been added. Always follow one set of measurements only, never mix metric and imperial.

PART ONE

JAMS, JELLIES, CONSERVES, MARMALADES AND CURDS

1

JARS, COVERS
AND EQUIPMENT

The choice of jar, the type of cover and the method of covering is most important.

The paramount feature is to seal down before mould, yeasts and germs have had time to get in and then to ensure complete and safe protection with a long-lasting, airtight cover which effectively prevents evaporation, fermentation, desiccation and general deterioration while in store.

The commercial processor exhausts the jar after filling, and then fits a completely airtight screw or half-turn metal or plastic cover which keeps the product thoroughly appetizing even after fairly long storage under widely varying and often unsuitable conditions.

It pays to buy the jars and fittings with screw or clip-on or half-turn caps and, after use, keep them carefully for 'next time'.

Jars and Tops

GLASS CAP, SCREW BAND
This is the old-style Kilner type jar from 225g (½ lb) upward which has a glass top and a screw band. It can be used for all types of processed foods including pickles and chutneys. The contents touch only glass.

SCREW CAP
This follows the common commercial pattern and has a ceresin or plastic lining or ring and a metal screw cap.

TWIST TOP
See page 15 and Fig. 1.

Fig. 1.   Three types of covers for jam.

Back: A twist top. This guarantees a long-lasting seal, and is the most
           reliable for centrally heated homes, or where storage space is
           near a heat source.
Middle: A plastic top.
Front: A waxed disc covered with a transparent cellophane cover.

As a final touch, carefully wash and dry each jar before labelling. For show
purposes, methylated spirit gives the outside of the jar sparkle.

THE HALF-TURN CAP OR SNAP-DOWN CAP
Usually of stiff plastic, it is efficient provided that it makes a
complete seal when snapped down. (All types do not effect an
airtight seal because of sizing, so be careful to check this when
buying.)

Plastic tops (see Fig. 1) placed on very hot jars form a
complete seal and become concave on cooling, and so do not

need a wax disc placed on top of the preserve.

GLASS JAM-JARS
A wax disc forms a seal on the surface of the jam and is placed on the top of the jar as soon as the jar is completely filled; either immediately or after the jam is cool, the top is cleaned and cellophane, parchment or cling film is placed on the jar to form a dust cover. Jam-jar tops vary in size and standard jam-jars are difficult to obtain.

HONEY JARS
These are not recommended, as a pocket of stale air can be trapped between the screw top and wax disc, leading to spoilage by mould growth.

Covers and Seals
Covers for jams, jellies and marmalades can be the 'breathing' type which consists of a moisture- and vapour-proof disc of waxed tissue. This is the actual seal and should be the correct size to cover the surface of the jam completely, but not adhere to the sides of the jar. The outer dust cover, usually transparent cellophane, should be put on when the preserve is either hot or cold, *never* when it is tepid or luke-warm, as moist air may cool and deposit moisture on the waxed disc, and this could possibly lead to spoilage during storage.

These waxed discs and dust covers (see Fig. 1) are the most popular method of sealing jams, jellies, marmalades and curds, and are generally sold in packets complete with rubber bands and labels. Cling film may be used as an *outer* dust cover for sugar preserves, and is best used double thickness. These covers are satisfactory in a clean, dry, cool and preferably dark storage cupboard for anything up to nine to twelve months. However, they are not wasp- or mouse-proof, and excessive heat, such as storage near a radiator, will cause shrinkage in the preserve.

Most commercial jams have a sealing lid of plastic-coated or lacquered metal. Somewhat similar *twist tops* are available for home use. These are widely used and can be bought from hardware shops and Women's Institute offices. As with plastic tops, a wax disc is not needed on top of the preserve.

These twist tops must not be used on fruit curds containing eggs, as curds do not reach the required temperatures (curds containing eggs will curdle if boiled). Use waxed discs, and either cellophane tissue covers or cling film. Packets of white plastic snap-on covers can also be bought, but they can only be used on the plain topped jam-jars, with no ridges or screw threads.

Lakeland Plastics, Kendal, Cumbria market these, and also a comprehensive range of equipment used in all methods of perservation.

Equipment

Apart from the usual appliances found in any efficient kitchen, there are others of special value:

BALANCE
One that is able to weigh the pan plus the cooking fruit.

BOTTLE BRUSHES
A special one to reach to the bottom of jars is needed.

BOWLS
Plenty of bowls are needed, for receiving the prepared fruit and vegetable and all the water. Plastic bowls are suitable if there is no acid in the ingredients, otherwise they should be made from earthenware, china, stainless steel, pyrex or non-chipped enamel.

CORER
Double ended for 1¾cm (⅝ in) and 2cm (¼ in) cores of apples and pears.

GRATER
Stainless steel.

JAR FILLER
Of heatproof glass, plastic or metal of a shape which allows for scooping up the hot jam without damage to the fingers.

JELLY BAG
Of flannel, butter muslin, cotton sheet, linen or cheese cloth, tied to the four legs of an upturned chair to form a jelly bag. Special jelly bags can be bought of 2.3 litre, 3.5 litre and 6.4 litre (2, 3 and 5½ quart) capacity and which are used on a special jelly bag stand.

LABELS
All sorts, gummed or self-adhesive.

LEMON SQUEEZER OR JUICE EXTRACTOR
Plastic or glass with strainer or electric squeezer.

MEASURE
1 litre graduated for ccs and pints and ozs, spoonfuls, etc.

METHYLATED SPIRIT
For testing the pectin quantity of the cooking fruit. Also, gives sparkle when rubbed on the outside of jars; this looks attractive when you are exhibiting your produce.

MUSLIN
For making a bag to hold pips, kernels, etc., during cooking.

PACKING SPOON
A long-handled, small-bowled, wooden spoon for assisting close-packing into jars.

PEELER
Stainless steel, either single or double-sided.

PRESERVING PAN
Stainless steel, enamel (uncracked); not iron or zinc. Brass and copper are good for green produce, but not for those which are red or highly acid. For effective rapid boiling, the pan should be wide and shallow.
   A pressure cooker can be used for smaller quantities.

SIEVE
Used for preliminary straining before putting through a fine strainer. Best made of nylon.

SKIMMER
Flat, perforated or slotted, wide spoon for removing stones or scum from jam, etc.

SPOON (STIRRING)
A long wooden spoon is preferred (so that you can stir without the hot jam splashing up), with a square or pointed end (not round) and with a 'stop' on the handle to prevent the spoon sliding down into the product.

STERILIZER

Bottles or jars which need sterilizing can be placed in any deep pan provided it is deep enough to cover the tops of the tallest bottles/jars with the water. A trivet, wooden base or folded newspaper should be placed on the base of the pan to prevent the bottles/jars from cracking.

STONE BASKET

Tinned-wire basket for hanging stones and kernels inside the pan when cooking to extract flavour; used as a receptacle when collecting stones from the hot jam.

STONER

For removing stones from cherries, peaches, apricots, plums and damsons. After the fruit skins are softened and the jam is the right texture, the sugar is added. Then any stones (e.g. in damson jam) will quickly rise to the surface and can be easily removed with the stoner.

Stones can also be removed by sieving just before the sugar is added.

THERMOMETER

A sugar boiling thermometer which is metal-cased and registers from 10°C (50°F) to 204°C (400°F) is suitable.

2

THE PRINCIPLES OF SUCCESSFUL JAM MAKING

What is a Jam?

It is a prepared fruit cooked to a precise formula so that the natural pectin and acid are extracted and, together with added sugar, forms a colourful and tasteful mixture which sets well and keeps for a long time.

A GOOD JAM possesses the following qualities:

1. Firm in consistency.
2. Brilliant in colour.
3. Even in fruit distribution.
4. Soft in texture of skin and flesh.
5. True flavour of the fruit.
6. Filled to the jar top.
7. Capable of storage without the formation of syrup, crystals, mould or ferment.

A POOR JAM:

1. Is runny or stiff.
2. Dull in colour, i.e. too light or too dark.
3. Uneven of texture, i.e. fruit particles at bottom as a layer or at top as a float.
4. Has hard skin or flesh (not cooked).
5. Is lacking or masking the true flavour.
6. Is not filled to the top.
7. Deteriorates in store by becoming syrupy, forming sugar crystals, developing a mould, or by turning to wine or vinegar.

It might be useful to learn these qualities or imperfections as they illustrate in a simple form the operation of processing.

The Practical Programme

Here are the simple but necessary operations:

1. Select.
2. Prepare.
3. Weigh and place in pan.
4. Add water (if required).
5. Add acid.
6. Simmer to cook.
7. Test for pectin (the setting agent).
8. Add pectin.
9. Add sugar off the heat. Make sure that sugar has dissolved.
10. Boil rapidly.
11. Stir.
12. Test for setting.
13. Skim.
14. Fill jars.
15. Seal.
16. Label.
17. Store.

Operation 1 – Select

The fruit should be *firm* and *just ripe*. If it is over-ripe, the setting quality is reduced.

It should be fresh so that no flavour is lost or colour deteriorated. It should be *disease-free* (especially if purchased) in order to avoid waste and preparation time.

It should be dry, otherwise calculations may be upset by the amount of extra water within the pulp and/or adhering to the skin.

If a variety is known to be low in pectin, then add 20% of that same fruit in an unripe condition. (See Operation 7 for the pectin rule.)

Operation 2 – Prepare

Soiled large fruits should be wiped over; small fruits washed briskly by running water through a colander in which they are placed.

Discard decayed, squashy, over-ripe, small, hard, or green fruits. Selected red, white and black currants should be stalked; pears and apples peeled, cored, sliced and quartered; strawberries, raspberries and blackberries de-stalked when necessary; stoned fruits either left whole or stoned before or after cooking; cherry, bullace, damson, sloe, stoned; gooseberries top and tailed; rhubarb trimmed into sticks to fit the jar or cut into 1½cm (¾ in) cubes.

Plums, apricots, peaches and nectarines can be peeled, halved, the stones removed, a few cracked open and the kernels put back into the jam for flavour; but not in excess of six kernels per 450g (1 lb) jar or the flavour may be too pronounced.

Operation 3 – Weigh and Pan

If the method requires the weight to be considered during processing, then the empty pan must be weighed at the start using a firm balance to avoid any accident when the pan contains the cooking fruit or jam.

By weighing, one can then deduct the pan weight later when it is necessary to calculate the weight of the fruit, sugar and jam during cooking.

To ensure the important speedy boiling at the finish, the depth in the pan of the fruit, water and sugar should not exceed 15cm (6 in).

To reduce the formation of sugar scum, smear over the inside of the pan bottom 15g (½ oz) of butter or cooking margarine or pour in one teaspoonful of glycerine to each 1.8kg (4 lb) of fruit. The pan should be wide and shallow. Stainless steel pans are excellent. Enamel pans without inside chips are satisfactory.

Brass and copper pans (so often used) are good especially for greengages and green gooseberries to hold the colour, but not for red or acid fruits. Copper pans are likely to destroy vitamin C in such rich fruits as rose-hips, black currants, strawberries, oranges and lemons, peaches, red or white currants, grapefruit, pineapple and tomatoes – in descending order of merit.

Operation 4 – Add Water

None, little or much water is added at the beginning of the cooking for these reasons:

1. To extract the fruit juices;
2. To collapse the cell walls and release the 'jellying' pectin;
3. To soften the skins;
4. To prevent scorching or burning of the fruits at the pan bottom.

Use soft water if available.

HOW MUCH WATER?

Here is a rough indication of the amount of water required for different fruits, but always check individual recipes for exact quantities.

None for juicy fruits, such as raspberries, elderberries, loganberries and strawberries; *half volume* (half as much water as there is fruit) for stiff-textured fruits such as plums, greengages, rhubarb and apples; *equal volume* for hard-textured fruit, such as black currants (tough skin), quinces, medlars and pears; *two or three volumes* for citrus fruits, such as oranges, lemons, grapefruit and limes.

Use rather less water if the fruit is ripe or gathered wet; more water for a very shallow pan as evaporation is more rapid.

If *insufficient water* is added, the fruit will not be soft, the pectin will not be released, skins will remain hard, and scorching may spoil the flavour and colour.

If *too much water* is added, the juice will be weak and may need much cooking to evaporate it, with consequent loss of colour.

Operation 5 – Add Acid

The jam must have acid, pectin and sugar in the correct proportion to give a good set.

The acidity of the fruit can be roughly gauged by comparing the tartness or sourness with a mixture of one tablespoonful of fresh lemon juice (or ¼ teaspoonsful of tartaric acid) dissolved in half a cup of water.

When tasted, if the fruit seems as acid as the lemon juice then no more need be added; if it is sweeter, then acid will be required. Acid also brightens up the colour.

ACID-LACKING FRUITS

These are sweet ripe apples, unripe bananas, bilberries, blackberries (early blackberries contain some acid; late ones have none), cherries (cooking or sweet unripe ones, not Morello cherries), figs, marrows, medlars, melons, nectarines, peaches, pears (especially ripe, dessert ones), pumpkins, quinces, raspberries and strawberries.

ADDING ACID

There are three proven good schemes:

1. 150ml (¼ pint) gooseberry or red currant juice;

    or

2. Two tablespoonfuls of lemon juice;

    or

3. An acid solution made by dissolving one level teaspoonful of tartaric acid or citric acid in half a teacup of water.

Before cooking, one of the above is added to each 1.8kg (4 lb) fruit in the pan and stirred round.

Operation 6 – Cook

The fruit, plus any water, plus any acid, should be brought slowly to the boil and then the heat turned down to a slow and long simmering (according to the fruit variety), the purpose being to:

1. Cook the fruit;
2. Draw out the juice;
3. Soften the flesh and skin;
4. Extract the pectin;
5. Evaporate any excess of water (according to the recipe);
6. Concentrate the fruit pulp so as to avoid the need for prolonged boiling after the sugar is added.

HOW LONG TO COOK?

The condition of the cooking fruit should be inspected frequently. Cooking will normally be sufficient when the flesh, tissues and skins are soft. Soft fruits like raspberries will take 10–15 minutes; medium-stiff fruits like plums 25–30 minutes; hard fruits like pears or with tough skins like black currants 40–45 minutes.

It is *important* to simmer long *before* the sugar is added or the too early 'sugaring' will harden the skins and flesh, after which further cooking will not make any improvement.

It may be necessary to simmer longer than usual if:

1. The fruit is unripe or wet;
2. The intensity of heat is low;
3. The pan is deep and its contents are deeper than 12cm (5 in).

USING A HOT PLATE
With an electric or an Aga or Rayburn stove which has a flat hot plate, the jam pan should also have a flat base so that the heat can be freely transferred from plate to pan.

If this is not the case, then the cooking may well be slow and long. Assuming a proper pan is used, the electric switch should be set to low and the simmering plate on the side of the Aga or Rayburn used.

USING A PRESSURE COOKER
A pressure cooker can be used both to cook the fruit and as an open pan when the sugar has been added, provided that the pan is not more than half-full.

Always consult the manufacturer's book of instructions before starting on any method of preservation.

Pressure cooking is usually at 4½kg (10 lb)/medium pressure for 1–10 minutes, according to the variety of fruit used. After allowing the required time, remove the pressure cooker from the source of heat and allow the pressure to reduce at room temperature.

Operation 7 – Test for Pectin
If a jam is to set well and keep long, it MUST contain enough pectin, and a simple test should be made to see if there is sufficient; and if not, to add some.

The fruit is cooked to the appropriate time when the following test is carried out. One teaspoonful of the clear cooked fruit juice is placed in a cold tumbler or cup and allowed to cool for 1 minute, then 3 teaspoonfuls of methylated spirit are poured in and shaken up. It is left for 1 minute and then poured gently into another vessel.

If there is *plenty* of pectin, one transparent lump will have formed; if only *sufficient*, two or four small clots will be seen which can be broken up into further blobs; if *too little* is present, the clots will be many, small and weak. Cook further in the hope of extracting more pectin or, which is better, add extra pectin to the cooking fruit.

Pectin is *low* and required in *considerable* quantities for sweet ripe cherries, ripe figs, vegetable marrows, pears, pumpkins, ripe peaches, rhubarb and strawberries; in *moderate* amounts for sweet apples, bananas, blackberries, cooking cherries, elderberries, medlars, nectarines, peaches, raspberries and tomatoes.

Operation 8 – Add Pectin
HOW TO ADD PECTIN
There are four ways by adding:

1. Home-made pectin.
2. Pectin-rich fruit.
3. Lemon peel (and pith).
4. Commercially-made pectin.

1. Home-made Fruit Juice Pectin
Make this from an extract of green gooseberries, red currants or green apples. Place the prepared fruit in a pan and to each 1.8kg (4 lb) add 900ml (1½ pints) water. Simmer until tender and strain. Next day, return the pulp to the pan and add 450ml (¾ pint) water to each 1.8 kg (4 lb) of fruit used at the start. Simmer for one hour, strain and then add both extracts together.

Store this extract in a screw-band or spring-clip covered jar. Sterilize it by standing the jar in a pan of boiling water for 5 minutes. See pages 18 and 113. Then seal airtight.

In fruits deficient in pectin, add 300ml (½ pint) of this extract to each 1.8kg (4 lb) of fruit; for fruits fairly low in pectin, add 150ml (¼ pint) and stir. Test for pectin and add a further quantity if the 'clot' is still weak.

2. Pectin-rich Fruit
The low pectin quantity can be boosted by the addition, before cooking, of fruits rich in pectin, such as green apples, crab apples, bullaces, black currants, red and white currants, damsons, green gooseberries, unripe grapes, loganberries, oranges (bitter, in pith) and quinces.

Thus suitable combinations would be cherry and apple, raspberry and red currant, blackberry and apple, rhubarb and loganberry, strawberry and red currant, pumpkin and bullace, pear and gooseberry – the fruit which is lacking pectin being given first.

3. Lemon Peel

The white pith contains the pectin, so the peel should be finely sliced (and, if not required in the final jam, suspended in a muslin bag and removed later) and added at the rate of 4 lemons per 1.8kg (4 lb) fruit at the *beginning* of the cooking.

If the fruit is *also* deficient in acid, slice the peel *and* include the juice as well, e.g. for sweet cherries, ripe figs, marrows, peaches and dessert pears.

4. Commercial Pectin

This is bought, either in powder or liquid form, complete with instructions. It is added after the sugar is added and the whole pan has been brought up to rapid boiling for the time stated in the instructions. When the pan is taken from the heat, the pectin is stirred into the jam and potted off.

Usually 1.4kg (3 lb) sugar, 1kg (2 lb) fruit (e.g. strawberries) and the pectin (150ml/¼ pint to 1.8kg/4 lb of fruit or as advised) will yield 2¼kg (5 lb) of jam but the colour and flavour are rather different from jam made with the help of pectin from other complementary fruits.

Operation 9 – Add Sugar

It matters little whether the sugar is cane or beet, or, indeed, whether it is preserving, castor, lump or granulated. Brown sugar may be used on dark fruits as it will tend to darken colour further and it also gives a distinct and not unpleasant flavour. Taking all in all, granulated sugar seems to be highly satisfactory. The cheapest is as good as the most expensive.

HOT SUGAR
The sugar should be heated in an oven for these reasons:

1. To avoid lowering the temperature of the cooking fruit;
2. To return the jam to boiling quickly;
3. To evaporate any moisture which might weaken the setting; and
4. To avoid possible later crystallization, especially when the acid and pectin contents are high.

When the fruit pulp is cooked thoroughly to tenderize and to extract the pectin, remove the pan from the source of the heat

then add the sugar gradually and stir in to dissolve. Following this, the jam should be brought up to boiling point rapidly.
If the sugar is added too soon:

1. Skins and flesh are hardened and withstand softening;
2. Too little water is driven off and the jam will not keep;
3. Further boiling to drive off water will destroy the pectin, and setting will be prevented; and
4. The jam is darkened and its flavour diminished.

The *important feature* at this junction is to simmer long and slow before the sugar is added and boil rapidly after the sugar is added.

HOW MUCH SUGAR TO ADD?
This depends upon the quantity of pectin (as shown by the clot test): the greater the amount of pectin, the more sugar can be used to produce firm jam, of full flavour and likely to keep well.

If the pectin test shows a very good clot, add 675g (1½ lb) of sugar to each 450g (1 lb) of fruit or to each 600ml (1 pint) of juice. If a good clot, add 450g (1 lb) of sugar. If a poor clot, add 350g (¾ lb) of sugar.

Normally, a long-keeping jam will contain 60% of added sugar and 5% of its own natural sugar. If it contains more, it may crystallize; if less, it may ferment and go 'winey' or form mould. Two-and-a-quarter kilos (5 lb) of jam are normally produced from 1.4kg (3 lb) of sugar.

Operation 10 – Boil Rapidly
When all the added sugar is dissolved, heat as rapidly as possible up to 'rolling boil', i.e. one which continues to bubble even when it is stirred.

This is to concentrate the sugar, pectin and acid and to reach a point when, on cooling, the jam will make a firm set.

Boiling should continue until tests show that the setting point has been reached. Further boiling will pass the setting point and will result in a sticky jam.

Operation 11 – Stir
The sugar is stirred into the fruit to dissolve it completely. However, continuous stirring is not recommended as it usually

forces bubbles down and submerges the scum. Just stir it sufficiently to prevent any jam being stuck and burnt onto the bottom of the pan.

Operation 12 – Test For Setting
Boiling is continued until the jam has reached a point when it will set and keep well; this point has to be found so that the boiling can be stopped. Further boiling will turn the jam into a thick mass which will not set or will set 'solid'.

There is a choice of one of five tests:

1. Cold plate;
2. Flake;
3. Weight;
4. Volume; and
5. Temperature.

N.B. While any tests are being made, pull the pan off the heat or boiling may progress too far.

1. COLD PLATE TEST
A small teaspoonful of the liquid part of the jam is poured onto a cold saucer or plate (which has been in the freezing part of the fridge for half an hour).

The jam will cool quickly and the edge of the jam is then pushed slightly with a teaspoon or with a finger-nail. If the surface easily wrinkles and feels stiff, then it can safely be potted off; if it still flows freely and is thin, then further boiling is necessary.

2. FLAKE TEST
A wooden spoon is dipped into the jam to collect up a liquid part, taken out, and allowed to cool quickly in a draught. The spoon is then turned slowly over to see how the jam falls off the edge.

If a 'flake' is formed by the thick liquid running together and it falls off slowly and cleanly, boiling is complete; if several thin flakes run off quickly (see Fig. 3 page 30), then further boiling is needed.

Fig. 2.   The Cold Plate Test.
A spoonful of hot jam is placed on a cold plate (from the fridge), allowed to thicken for half a minute and then pushed with a finger nail. If (as shown) it is stiff and crinkles, then the jam can be potted.

3.   WEIGHT TEST

This is satisfactory for most types of jam and relies upon the fact that a good-keeping jam contains 60% added sugar. Thus there is 3 lb sugar to 2 lb fruit in 5 lb of jam.

The jam and spoon must be weighed at the start and allowed for in the weighing of the boiling jam in this test. The weight should be calculated by multiplying by five and dividing by three the weight of sugar added; if the jam weight is 5 lb (or proportionally) then setting point has been reached.

4.   VOLUME TEST

This is a method to calculate approximately the weight of the

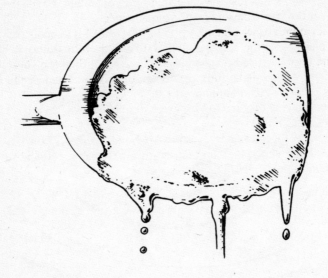

Fig. 3.   The Flake Test.
This jam, in the process of boiling, runs off the wooden spoon in several thin streams and must therefore continue to be boiled until it is thicker and runs off in a single sheet or flake when it must be potted at once.

jam from its volume, gauged by a notched stick or spoon handle.

Prior to making the jam, into the empty pan is poured one 450g (1 lb) jam-jar full of water; the water height is marked on the stick, held vertically on the pan bottom.

A further jam-jar full of water is poured in and the stick marked. This is repeated to the top of the pan, numbering each mark.

A simple calculation (see 'weight' above) will tell the boiling-out weight of the properly boiled jam and this is read off on the stick, having allowed the bubbling to cease. If the level is above the mark, then boiling must continue and further tests made until satisfactory.

5.   TEMPERATURE TEST

Although precise, it may be advisable to confirm with the flake or plate test as this test only registers the percentage of sugar. Over-boiling is troublesome with some recipes.

A thermometer which goes up to 115°C (240°F) is needed and this is placed into the boiling jam and stirred carefully round.

If the temperature is shown as 104°C (220°F), then the sugar quantity is adequate so long as the amounts of acid and pectin were provided at the commencement.

If the flake test seems to 'disagree', it may be wise to boil on to 105°C (222°F).

Keep the thermometer in a pan of boiling water when not being used to check the jam temperature. After use, return the thermometer to the boiling water.

Operation 13 – Skim

It is wasteful to stir the scum during the boiling: better to wait

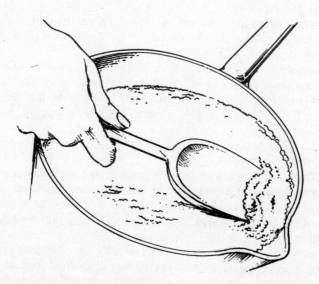

Fig. 4.   Skimming.
Removing sugar scum from the boiling jam prior to potting.

until completed. Use either a wooden spoon, a plastic spatula or a perforated ladle spoon. Edge the scum to the side then scoop up and over.

Pouring a teaspoonful of butter or oil on the scum in the pan can disperse some of the scum.

Operation 14 – Fill Jars

The jars of any shape or size must be properly clean, dry and perferably hot (by placing in an oven or on the top of a stove or in front of a fire).

Use white glass jars which have no commercial labels on them and are undamaged. Honey and coffee jars with a cardboard disc inside their lids are not recommended as they encourage mould growth.

As soon as the setting point is reached, draw the pan from the source of heat and fill up the jars at once. To avoid soiling the jars, a special wide funnel should be used, as well as a mug which is able to take at least 450g (1 lb) of jam at a time to save dripping and spilling.

It is important to fill almost to the jar rim because shrinkage after cooling will reduce the level down to ½cm or 1cm (¼ or ½ in) from the top.

When the fruit used is whole or partly so, it is well to allow some cooling (until a skin forms) before potting so that the density of the jam prevents the fruit from rising to the top. Such jams are strawberry, apple, ginger, marrow, pumpkin and marmalade.

Operation 15 – Seal

N.B. Immediately each jar is filled, place on the hot jam surface a waxed circle or disc (waxed side down) so that it lays flat on the jam surface excluding air beneath it, and fits flush to the jar sides. This checks the growth of mould whilst the jam is being stored.

Generally, the most satisfactory results are obtained by *sealing airtight immediately each very hot jar is filled* (one at a time, keeping the others hot). A wooden board is ideal for standing the hot jars on: wood is a poor conductor of heat and therefore the jars keep hot.

Twist tops or plastic tops effect a quick and definite seal and

Fig. 5.   Sealing.
Immediately the hot jam is poured almost to the top in the hot jars, it is covered with the right size waxed paper circle (the wax side downward), after which the cover is fitted airtight.

so do not need a wax disc placed on top of the preserve.

A cheaper and good seal is that of cellophane (see Fig. 6) or parchment sheet circle, pressed over and tied with a double round of thin string or secured with a stout rubber band (supplied in packets of cellophane jam pot covers).

If there is a history of mould or surface deterioration, an excellent precaution is to dip the covers or discs in surgical spirit, the surplus being shaken off before fixing.

Operation 16 – Label
Labels can be home-made, cut from 25cm × 20cm (10 in × 8 in) sheets of gummed paper or bought ready-made. They can be plain, bordered, white, coloured, pictured, square, oval or round – choose whatever you like and looks most attractive.

Fig. 6.   Covering a jar.
A cheap and easy method of covering a jar using cellophane.

Some plastic labels refuse to adhere until the jars are cold.

The labels should include the name of the jam and the date it was made. Helpful brief details of manufacture can be put on the labels or in a little book, kept for the purpose.

If one is exhibiting, points are lost for untidiness and for using an unauthorized label. Old labels can usually be removed with an application of nail varnish remover, methylated spirits, white spirits or cleaning fluid.

Operation 17 – Store
This is important and a place (room or cupboard) in the house or out-buildings should be found which is cool, frost-proof, dry, dark, airy, wasp- and mouse-free. A damp place will lead to

mould attacking the cover and the disc; exposure to light will spoil colour brilliancy; a warm cupboard will encourage evaporation and shrinkage; a frosty loft may split the jars.

Tracing Mistakes

MOULD (MILDEW)

Loose-fitting cap; damp storage (especially with adhesive cover); sealing when warm (should be very hot) and so enclosing mould spores; sugar content below 60%; thin liquid consistency.

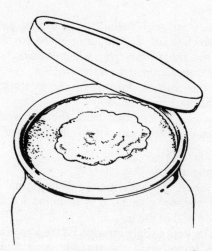

Fig. 7. Mould.
An example of mould growth spreading on the top surface of the jam.

SUGAR CRYSTALS

Too long boiling and thus high sugar content; early adding of too much sugar; adding of acid after adding sugar; long cooking to make long and soft crystals of invert sugar; insufficient acid when crystals are sucrose and are hard, gritty and granulated; chemical failure or the sugar (sucrose) to be hydrolized (converted) into levulose and destrose sugar.

POOR SET
Fruit not cooked long enough to extract the natural pectin; low pectin content of fruit which requires assistance; not sufficient water evaporated off during cooking; too ripe fruit when pectin has lost its value; boiling too long after sugar added; too much sugar added in proportion to acid and pectin; severe lack of acid.

SYRUPY
If long over-boiling takes place after the sugar is added, a sticky mass of caramelised syrup can result. The use of over-ripe fruit can also produce this.

FERMENTATION
Small bubbles are seen within the jam-jars; yeasts are acting upon jam which is not set firm, pointing to an insufficient sugar content or too short simmering when cooking to reduce water content; not covered airtight; warm storage.

Bubbles can also be formed at the potting if the jam is allowed to become quite tepid.

(This jam can be emptied from the jars and boiled up to increase sugar content, re-potted in hot jars and used for cooking.)

UNEVEN DISTRIBUTION
With jams where particles remain distinguishable (e.g. straw-berries and marrow ginger), it is common for these pieces to rise to the top half of the jar.

They can be kept evenly arranged if the jam is allowed to cool until a skin forms upon the surface, after which the jam is stirred to distribute the particles and then potted.

It is advisable to dip the wax circle and the cover in surgical spirit before fixing in order to kill mould, etc.

SHRINKAGE
Not filling jars up to the top; use of covers which are not airtight or which leak air in warm or damp storage.

The Best Sorts of Fruits

If it is possible to grow or purchase and use the most suitable varieties, then the result will be superior in flavour and colour than otherwise, but where the price comes into the picture, it is right and proper to jam what you can grow or obtain cheaply.

APPLES

Bramley's Seedling is the best all round. Lord Derby cooks down to a dull crimson. Monarch makes good jam. Dessert varieties are not good cookers and have too little acid.

APRICOTS

Moorpark seems to be the only good one available. It has orange-red flesh and an excellent flavour when some of the kernels are cooked with the fruit.

BLACKBERRIES

For cultivated sorts, the Himalaya Giant ripens early and is nicely acid. Fantasia, a recent introduction, is a large and heavy-cropping cultivar of good flavour. The most suitable wild sorts are those which fruit early, being the most juicy and acid. Late blackberries are of little value. Ashton Cross has a very good flavour.

CHERRIES

The red cooking varieties are to be recommended: Morello, May Duke and Kentish Red. On the other hand, jam any which are handy and cheap. Black cherries are colourful. Remember the need for both acid and pectin.

CURRANTS, BLACK

Most sorts jam well, pride of place going to Boskoop Giant, Baldwin and Seabrooks; and Ben Alder and Ben Lomond are noted for their processing value.

CURRANTS, RED

The best all round is Laxtons No. 1. Stanza, Redstart and Jonkheer Vantets are newer cultivars.

CURRANTS, WHITE

Although colour is missing, these are useful to provide acid and pectin to other fruit of which the colour is to be retained. White Versailles and White Grape are both good sorts.

DAMSONS

An excellent jam-maker; good varieties being Merryweather (true flavour), Farleigh (black) and Bradley's King (sweet). Early Rivers has very good flavour.

FIGS
The only one which jams well is Brown Turkey, but it needs both acid and pectin.

GOOSEBERRIES
Most sorts (when young green) are high in acid and pectin and useful to add to other fruits. The choice is as follows: Langley Gage, Keepsake and Howard's Lancer (all green when ripe for green jam); Lancashire Lad, Whinham's Industry (super-excellent for jam), Crown Bob (all red); Careless (another super), Whitesmith and White Lion (white when ripe); Leveller, Early Sulphur, Golden Drop (three best used for dessert, yellow).

GRAPES
Any available cheap; white, red or black or ornamental.

LOGANBERRIES
Make an excellent jam full of flavour and colour – as do the hybrid brambles such as Boysenberry, Tayberry, Tummelberry and Sunberry. Contain more acid and pectin than raspberries.

MELON
Charentais (perfumed orange), Sweetheart (salmon pink) both cantaloup.

MULBERRIES
Must be fresh as they quickly go mouldy. The black mulberry is the one to choose.

NECTARINES
Only if you grow them or get them from a friend. The best all round is Lord Napier (white flesh), but the best for colour is River's Orange (rich orange).

ORANGES
Any sort according to the type of marmalade and whether solo or in mixture.

PEACHES
Only if given or exchanged! Choose those with rich colour and free stone, e.g. Hale's Early and Rochester.

PEARS
Poor in acid and pectin. Choice is on jam quality, colour and availability; Jargonelle (musky), William's (the Bartlett for

canning); Beurre Hardy (rose-water), Conference (pink flesh), Pitmaston Duchess (cooks well), Glou Morceau (delicious flavour), and Catillac (the cooking pear, amber red).

PLUMS

A popular jam. Any sort do well, but watch progress when cooking. Here is a choice: Czar (purple), Oullin's Gage (golden), Pershore Yellow Egg plum and Purple Egg (suitable for good jam), Victoria (red yellow, popular) and Marjorie's Seedling (black, late). Sweet dessert sorts are not so suitable.

QUINCES

Quince jelly – lovely! Rich flavour. Little acid but ample pectin. Any are good, especially the Portugal for flavour.

RASPBERRIES

These vary in flavour. The choice being Malling Promise, Norfolk Giant (old but one of the best), Glen Moy, Glen Prosen, Admiral and Leo.

RHUBARB

Best for colour and flavour are Champagne and Cawood Delight. It does not matter much; all are good, but especially those rather more mature and cheaper in summer as they set better, although they can be deficient in both acid and pectin and should be tested.

STRAWBERRIES

If you have a choice, then for flavour it is the old Royal Sovereign with the scarlet colour, for quantity it is Cambridge Favourite (of regular shape and relatively long-standing qualities), for freezing Totem. Elsanta, Hapil and Tenira are all of good flavour.

TOMATOES

Either red or yellow; medium-sized globular fruit rather than odd-shaped; must be fully ripe and coloured, but not too liquid inside. Have hardly any pectin.

Adding Flavour

It would not be sensible or practical to add chemical flavour. If the jam is made 'properly', the flavour of the fruit will be obvious and pleasant.

However some fruits are not, in themselves, possessed of a robust flavour, and the general attraction of such a jam is improved by the addition of another fruit which will act as a complementary support.

Here are some mixtures which blend well:

apple with ginger or blackberry or date or cherry or clove or lemon or mulberry;

carrot with almond or gooseberry or lemon;

cherry with gooseberry or loganberry or apricot or red currant;

cucumber with ginger or orange;

marrow with ginger or pineapple or blackberry or damson or quince;

melon with lemon;

pear with ginger or orange or clove or cinnamon;

rhubarb with damson or black currant or raspberry or loganberry or orange.

Adding Colour

Although the professional processors use much flavour and colour, the chemicals are under the control of the Department of Health. It is a highly specialized branch and not to be adopted by home jam-makers.

On the other hand, as with flavour, certain fruits and certain varieties of those fruits possess natural colouring which, when blended and added to a fruit which has little colour, will quite clearly improve the final preserve.

Fruits which are good for colouring are: damsons, blue and purple plums, blackberries, black currants, red currants (some sorts), mulberries and loganberries.

Fruits which lack colour and can well be improved are: pears, apples, white heart cherries, white currants, yellow raspberries, some plums, japonica, marrow and some peaches.

Sugar Saving

Sugar is costly and cannot be consumed heavily by some people. It is interesting then to see what sort of a jam can be made with less sugar than normal. Flavour is usually especially pronounced.

It *can* be made successfully so long as:

1. There is *ample* acid and pectin (natural or commercial) in the final boiling.
2. 225g–350g (½–¾ lb) of sugar is added to each 450g (1 lb) of fruit.
3. Testing is done by flake or plate test (the weight or temperature test would lead to much boiling resulting in no saving in sugar for the weight of jam made).
4. Setting point – should be watched and may well be reached earlier than usual; start testing after 5 minutes' hard boiling.
5. *Important*. As soon as ready, the hot jam should be poured (without delay) into hot jars and sealed *airtight* at once with twist top or plastic covers.

IN PLACE OF SUGAR

Sugar (sucrose), an essential constituent of a jam, along with acid and pectin, ensures a good set, top flavour and long keeping. Other sweet substances have good and bad features.

Honey

This is expensive and gives much of its own flavour. It can replace a quarter of the sugar (half at the most), but the boiling time must be watched and limited or crystals will be formed. This jam has a soft set. Honey is not satisfactory for whole fruit conserves.

Treacle

Has a distinct flavour; otherwise follow the suggestions under 'Honey'.

Glucose

This is expensive, does not sweeten as much as sucrose and has no particular attribute. It may replace a quarter of the sugar, but has a tendency to darken the jam. There is a risk of mould developing.

Saccharine

Its only value is its ability to sweeten. It has no value as a setting agent.

Salt

This is an economy measure. For each 450g (1 lb) of fruit add

100g (4 oz) of sugar into which is mixed one teaspoonful of salt. Cook and boil as usual, but pot hot and airtight.

It can be stiffened by adding (after the salt and sugar) 15g (½ oz) seed pearl barley soaked overnight.

SUGAR-LESS JAM (DIABETIC)

Glycerine and Saccharine
The fruit is prepared and cooked by simmering. For each 1.8 kg (4 lb) of fruit is stirred in 30–35 ⅓rd grain (0.3 grain) saccharine tablets (dissolved in hot water) and 1.6 litres (2⅔ pints) glycerine (1.15 litres/2 pints for 1.4kg/3 lb fruit).

The mixture is then brought to boiling until it becomes thick (the setting test is not possible) when it is put hot into hot jars, preferably with a twist top or plastic lid and sealed airtight.

Gelatine and Saccharine
Cook the fruit as usual and add: a solution of 50g (2 oz) of powdered gelatine in 300ml (½ pint) of boiling water, plus 30–35 ⅓rd grain (0.3 grain) saccharine tablets (in hot water).

Bring to boil and boil for 5 minutes, then pour into hot jars, put on the covers loosely, place in a water bath (see page 113) and sterilize by boiling for 5 minutes. Then seal airtight.

It is well to use small jars for these jams so that mould can be controlled.

Pectin-base Jams

Commercial pectins are quite safe (normally made from apples or lemons) and are valuable for getting a good set with fruits low in pectin, e.g. strawberries.

Instructions should be followed because an excess is uneconomical, wasteful and tends to mask flavour and weaken colour. However, a greater weight of jam is produced because the long boiling (to extract pectin) is avoided.

A recommended method is:

1. Prepare fully ripe fruit;
2. Weigh fruit, add usual water and simmer until cooked;
3. Add sugar (as usual) and mix well;
4. Bring to rapid boiling for 2 minutes (or according to manufacturers' instructions);

5. Take pan from heat, stir in the pectin;
6. Cool if advised;
7. Pot and seal hot.

This improves on keeping; ideally for a month.

Vegetable Jams

These jams follow the general rules for fruit jams, except that they contain no acid or pectin – which must be added or the jams will neither set nor keep well.

Vegetables must be *fresh* so that the flavour is at its peak; *young* and tender; *disease-free* to avoid loss and waste; *right variety* to ensure good colour and flavour.

PREPARATION
Carrots
Cut, wash, peel, slice, cube or shred.

Cucumber
Peel and slice thinly.

Marrows and Pumpkins
Wash, remove seeds and cut into cubes or strips.

Tomatoes
Red: skinned and cut in halves. Green: thinly slice. To skin, dip in boiling water for half a minute, then dip into cold water.

The procedure for making vegetable jams follows that for making fruit jams, taking care to see that the acid and pectin are added either from home-made (see page 25) or commercial (page 26), or by mixing in a fruit which is rich in these two essentials (page 25).

It may also be well to consider the addition of flavour and colours (page 40).

VARIETIES
These have been carefully chosen (from experimental research) to give the best results, but cheap good produce should not be refused.

Beetroot
Crimson Globe (dark blood-red, sweet), Long Red (black-red), Golden (orange-yellow), Snow White (white).

Carrot
Autumn King (orange flesh), Chantenav (red), James' Intermediate (scarlet), Nantes (orange red).

Cucumber
King of the Ridge (outdoor), Burpee Hybrid Ridge (white flesh). These are not bitter; skin is tender and soft.

Gourd
Sweet Dumpling.

Marrow
Bush Green (dark green flesh); Bush White (creamy white); Bush Gold Nugget (orange-yellow); Trailing Delicious (bright yellow).

Pumpkin
Mammoth (yellow flesh).

Tomato
Gemini (scarlet, fleshy, sweet, few seeds); Moneymaker (popular, medium-sized, good quality); Golden Amateur (golden, medium-sized, thin skin).

Judging Your Own Jams

The ability to appraise quality in home-produce goes far towards improvement in the next batch. Judging at shows and exhibitions is an interesting and worthwhile task. Here is what a judge looks at and does:

1. Jar (size, style and shape) and label and sealing according to the schedule.
2. Clean and highly attractive, well filled.
3. Bright fruit colour (according to fruit variety).
4. Even distribution of fruit and absence of bubbles.
5. Open the jar and look for mould and proper fitting of wax circle.
6. Take off circle, press spoon on surface to feel any crystals.
7. Push spoon in to appreciate consistency (too soft, or too stiff).
8. Colour can be seen well by pushing a white plastic spoon or spatula down inside the sides of the jar; shown bright.

9. Spoon up some jam to note any fermentation or syrup.
10. Examine for soft texture of skins, flesh and peel.
11. Too many stone kernels included?
12. All this time, try to appreciate the aroma which should be fresh, pleasant and of the fruit.
13. Lastly, flavour – not too much at once – to discover true fruit flavour, satisfactory sweetness, clean to the palate, free from grittiness of juice or odd off-flavours. A mixed fruit jam should possess the flavours of each. It may be well to check up on likely faults (page 35) and jam qualities (page 19).

A SCORE CARD

A judge uses a score card to award points for each quality that a jam has. The points for the different qualities are added up to reach a total. This total is then compared with the totals of other score-carded jams. In this way, the judge is able to award positions of merit.

The following gives the maximum number of points awarded for each quality:

External Standard Container, Cover, Label, Appearance	1
Internal Standard Colour	5
Quality Consistency, Texture, Quantity	6
Flavour, Aroma	8
	——
	20

3

SUCCESSFUL JAM
RECIPES

FRUIT JAMS

All the recipes use 1.8kg (4 lb) fruit. The average yield with 1.8kg (4 lb) sugar is 3kg (6⅔ lb). Follow the programme as described in Chapter 2.

Apple

APPLE AND BLACK CURRANT
A purple 'apple' jam.

450g (1 lb) cooking apples, 1.4kg (3 lb) black currants, 2¼kg (5 lb) sugar, 900ml (1½ pints) water.

Cook the black currants in 600ml (1 pint) of water long and slow (testing every 10–20 minutes) so that the skins have been fully softened. Cook the prepared apples separately in 300ml (½ pint) of water to a firm pulp.

Add the black currants and apples together, and the sugar. Mix all well together, boil quickly, and pot hot.

APPLE AND BLACKBERRY (BRAMBLE)
1.4kg (3 lb) blackberries, 450g (1 lb) green cooking apples, 1.8kg (4 lb) sugar, 300ml (½ pint) water.

Cook the blackberries and apples slowly until soft. Add the sugar, boil to setting.

To produce *seedless* jam, cook the blackberries separately in 150ml (¼ pint) of water until the berries are soft. Then pass them through a coarse sieve to remove the pips. Cook the apples in the remaining 150ml (¼ pint) water and mix the apples and berries together. With this method, only 1.4kg (3 lb) sugar is needed.

APPLE AND ELDERBERRY

1kg (2 lb) apples, 1kg (2 lb) ripe elderberries, 300ml (½ pint) water, 1.8kg (4 lb) sugar, 2 lemons (pith, juice and grated rind).

Strip the berries from the stalk and sieve out the seeds after cooking. Simmer apples and elderberries together, add the sugar, boil hard and pot.

APPLE AND PLUM

It is popular and economical to use a heavy crop of each.

Equal quantities of each fruit, or as desired, to make 1.8kg (4 lb) in total, 1.8kg (4 lb) sugar, 600ml (1 pint) water.

Use cooking apples and preferably dark blue or purple plums. Peel and core the apples, stone the plums and weigh after this preparation to make up to 1.8kg (4 lb). Cook, add sugar and boil to setting.

APPLE AND RASPBERRY

A nice wine-red mixture.

1kg (2 lb) prepared cooking apples, 1kg (2 lb) hulled raspberries, 150ml (¼ pint) water, 2 lemons (pith and juice).

Cook the apples in the water to a firm pulp, add the raspberries, the lemon pith (in a muslin bag) and the lemon juice, stir in 1.8kg (4 lb) sugar, boil hard and pot hot.

APPLE CLOVE

Same as for *Apple Ginger* below, but use 10 cloves in place of the ginger.

APPLE GINGER

1.8kg (4 lb) apples, 1.7kg (3¾ lb) sugar, 700ml (1¼ pints) water, 2 level teaspoonfuls tartaric or citric acid *or* 8 tablespoonfuls lemon juice plus the rind (in a muslin bag), 175g (6 oz) preserved ginger (chopped fine) and 1 tablespoonful ground ginger.

Peel, core and slice the apples and put under the water and acid at once to stop browning. Put all this in the pan with the ground ginger. Cook, take out the bag, add the sugar and preserved ginger, stir boil to setting. This should yield nearly 3kg (6½ lb).

Apricot

APRICOT (FRESH)

1.8kg (4 lb) *fresh* apricots, 1.8kg (4 lb) sugar, 450ml (¾ pint) water, juice of 2 lemons.

Halve the fruit, remove the stones and add some blanched kernels (i.e. boiled in water to get the skins off them). Simmer all together until tender (takes quite a long time). Add the sugar, boil hard and pot.

APRICOT (DRIED)

Soak 1kg (2 lb) *dried* apricots in 3½ litres (6 pints) of water for 24 hours. Put all into the pan with 2 tablespoonfuls of lemon juice and simmer for 20 minutes. Add 2¾kg (6 lb) sugar, boil and pot. If liked, 100g (4 oz) of blanched shredded almonds can be put in with the sugar.

Black Currant

BLACK CURRANT

1.8kg (4 lb) currants (stripped off the stalks), 1¾ litres (3 pints) water, 2¾kg (6 lb) sugar.

(If you do not have sufficient black currants available but do have some red currants, you can use a mixture of black and red currants to make the jam, provided the total weight of currants adds up to 1.8kg (4 lb). You will not need so much water as red currants have a less tough skin than black currants.)

It is important to cook long and gently for 20–30 minutes until the skins are soft and the fruit can be pressed easily between the fingers.

Then add the sugar, stir well in to mix, boil hard and pot.

BLACK CURRANT AND APPLE

See *Apple and Black Currant*, page 46.

BLACK CURRANT AND RHUBARB

An economical jam using sliced rhubarb.

1kg (2 lb) of each fruit, 2kg (4½ lb) sugar.

Cook the fruit separately: the black currants in 600ml (1 pint) of water, the rhubarb in 300ml (½ pint) of water. Make sure the currants have been softened. Then mix them together, add the sugar, boil and pot.

Blackberry

BLACKBERRY

1.8kg (4 lb) blackberries, 1.8kg (4 lb) sugar, 150ml (¼ pint) water, 4 tablespoonfuls lemon juice, plus pith (in a muslin bag).

Simmer the berries and the lemon juice and the pith, add the sugar, boil hard and pot.

BLACKBERRY AND APPLE

See *Apple and Blackberry*, page 46.

BLACKBERRY AND ELDERBERRY

Both these wild fruits are free for collection and blend well together.

1kg (2 lb) each of the berries, 2kg (4 lb) sugar, juice and pith of 3 lemons. No water.

Cook slowly, with the lemon juice and pith, add the sugar, boil and pot.

If the combined cooked pulp is sieved, the seeds removed and 1.7kg (3½ lb) sugar is used, the result is most flavoursome.

Cherry

CHERRY

Choose May Duke or Morello for red colour; black cherries for a purple colour; white-heart for a pale cream colour. All cherries contain little acid and pectin.

1.8kg (4 lb) stoned cherries, 1.4kg (3 lb) sugar, 2¼ litres (4 pints) red currant or apple juice, juice and pith of 3 lemons.

Cook gently with the lemon and fruit juices until the halved cherries are tender, add the sugar, stir well, boil and pot.

CHERRY AND GOOSEBERRY

A pleasant mixture.

1.4kg (3 lb) stoned cherries (white-heart if you like), 450g (1 lb) green gooseberries (which turn red when ripe, see page 38), 1.8kg (4 lb) sugar, 300ml (½ pint) water.

Simmer the fruit together, add the sugar, boil and pot.

CHERRY AND LOGANBERRY

Another excellent flavour.

1kg (2 lb) stoned cherries, 1kg (2 lb) loganberries, 1.7kg (3¾lb) sugar, 300ml (½ pint) water.

Simmer, add sugar, boil and pot.

CHERRY AND RED CURRANT
If red cherries are used, the resultant colour is most pleasing.

1¼kg (2½ lb) stoned cherries, 675g (1½ lb) red currants, 1.7kg (3¾ lb) sugar, 300ml (½ pint) water.

Simmer the fruit together, add the sugar, boil and pot.

Damson

DAMSON
A delicious high-flavoured jam, easy to make.

1.8kg (4 lb) stoned damsons, 2¼kg (5 lb) sugar, 600ml (1 pint) water.

Alternatively the stones can be gathered off during cooking as they come to the top. Do not over-cook. Add the sugar, boil and pot.

DAMSON AND APPLE
See *Apple and Plum* (page 47).

Elderberry

ELDERBERRY
1.8kg (4 lb) stripped ripe berries, 1.6kg (3½ lb) sugar, no water, juice and pith of 3 lemons.

Simmer and sieve out the seeds when the fruit is soft. Add the lemon, boil and pot.

ELDERBERRY AND APPLE
See *Apple and Elderberry* (page 47).

ELDERBERRY AND BLACKBERRY
See *Blackberry and Elderberry* (page 49).

Gooseberry

GOOSEBERRY
An easy jam to make. It contains plenty of acid and pectin.

Choose the appropriate type of gooseberry for the colour jam you require. For varieties, see page 38. If you want a green jam, choose a gooseberry of the kind that is green when ripe, use a copper or brass pan and boil rather less than normal.

1.8kg (4 lb) gooseberries, 2¼kg (5 lb) sugar, 700ml (1¼ pints) water.

Simmer merely to soften the skins, not too much. Add the sugar, boil quickly, test early for setting and pot.

GOOSEBERRY AND CHERRY
See *Cherry and Gooseberry* (page 49).

GOOSEBERRY AND RED CURRANT
A very easy and delicious jam.

1kg (2 lb) gooseberries, 1kg (2 lb) red currants, 1.8kg (4 lb) sugar, 450ml (¾ pint) water.

Simmer all the fruit together to soften the skins; add the sugar, boil and pot.

GOOSEBERRY AND RHUBARB
A good setter and cheap.

1kg (2 lb) gooseberries (red when ripe), 1kg (2 lb) rhubarb (can be mature; the best to use is a red variety), 1.8kg (4 lb) sugar, no water.

Simmer all the fruit together, add the sugar, boil and pot.

GOOSEBERRY AND STRAWBERRY
1kg (2 lb) gooseberries (red when ripe, if possible), 1kg (2 lb) strawberries, 1.8kg (4 lb) sugar, 450ml (¾ pint) water (for cooking the gooseberries).

Cook the fruit separately and not over much. Add the sugar, boil and pot.

Greengage

GREENGAGE
This is listed here and not in the *Plum* section because the flavour and colour are usually superior. The most flavoursome and colourful gages are Oullin's (orange), Denniston's Superb (golden), Old Greengage (green) and Bryanston (deep orange).

1.8kg (4 lb) gages (stoned), 1.8kg (4 lb) sugar, 450ml (¾ pint) water if the gages are firm, 300ml (½ pint) if the gages are ripe.

The stones can be cracked and a few kernels included at the end of boiling.

Using a brass or copper pan will help the jam retain its green colour. Do not over-cook.

GREENGAGE AND APPLE
See *Apple and Plum* (page 47).

Loganberry

LOGANBERRY
A good setter with unique sharp flavour.

2kg (4 lb) sugar, 2kg (4 lb) loganberries. If the loganberries are over-ripe, add 1 tablespoonful lemon juice. No water.

Cook slowly until soft. Sieve out the seeds if desired. Add the sugar, boil quickly, test for setting and pot.

LOGANBERRY AND CHERRY
See *Cherry and Loganberry* (page 49).

LOGANBERRY AND RASPBERRY
Loganberry helps the raspberry to set, and the delicious aroma and flavour of both are pronounced.

1kg (2 lb) loganberries, 1kg (2 lb) raspberries, 1.8kg (4 lb) sugar, no water.

Cook the fruit slowly together until soft, not pappy. Sieving the pips out improves the final jam. Add the sugar, boil and pot.

LOGANBERRY AND RED CURRANT
A super-setting jam with a sharp flavour.

1kg (2 lb) loganberries, 1kg (2 lb) red currants, 1.8kg (4 lb) sugar, 450ml (½ pint) water (for cooking the red currants).

Cook the fruit separately; the loganberries do not need any water. Then mix them together, stir well, add the sugar, boil and pot.

Medlar

MEDLAR
A unique flavour well appreciated; little acid or pectin.

Cook until tender 2kg (4 lb) medlar and 1¾ litres (2½ pints) water, sieve and remove the husks.

To each 2kg (4 lb) of sieved pulp, add 1.7kg (3½ lb) sugar and the juice and pith of 4 lemons. Boil and pot.

Peach

PEACH
You may have an outdoor tree which bears prodigiously!

Remove the stones, and crack some for the kernels.

1.8kg (4 lb) peaches, 1.7kg (3¾ lb) sugar, 450ml (¾ pint) water, juice and pith of 4 lemons.

Do not over-cook. It is nice to see the shape of the fruit. Add the sugar, boil and pot.

PEACH AND PEAR
A useful combination.

1kg (2 lb) stoned and cubed peaches, 1kg (2 lb) ripe but firm pears cut into cubes, 2kg (4 lb) sugar, 450ml (¾ pint) water, juice and pith of 4 lemons.

Simmer all the fruit together, but do not over-cook. Add the sugar, boil and pot.

Pear

PEAR
Contains little acid or pectin.

1.8kg (4 lb) cooking pears, 1.7kg (3¾ lb) sugar, juice and pith of 4 lemons, 600ml (1 pint) water.

Stew the pears until tender with the lemon; this may take 30–40 minutes. Place them in the pan, add the sugar, boil and pot.

Pear jam by itself has no pronounced flavour so, if desired, you could add one of the following ingredients, before adding the sugar and before boiling:

25g (1 oz) root ginger (cut fine) or 1 dessertspoon ground ginger or the grated rind of 4 oranges or 450g (1 lb) tinned pineapple (cut fine – 1cm/½ in) or 450g (1 lb) clean stoned dates (cut fine – ½cm/¼ in).

If dessert pears are used, adopt the same procedure but only 300ml (½ pint) water will be required and the cooking time will be much reduced.

PEAR AND MARROW
See *Marrow and Pear* (page 59).

Plum

PLUM
An easy jam, quick to set and if not over-boiled has a most delicious flavour (see varieties on page 39).

2kg (4 lb) plums (stones removed and a few kernels put back), 2kg (4 lb) sugar, 600ml (1 pint) water (300ml/½ pint if very ripe plums are used).

Simmer the plums to cook them but not to a mushy pulp, merely to soften the skins. Add the sugar, boil and pot. Over-boiling will spoil the flavour and colour.

PLUM AND APPLE
See *Apple and Plum* (page 47).

PLUM AND ELDERBERRY
A pleasing combination of flavours.

1.4kg (3 lb) stoned plums, 450g (1 lb) elderberries (or 1kg/ 2 lb of each), 300ml (½ pint) water (for cooking the plums), 1.8kg (4 lb) sugar.

Cook each fruit separately, add them together, add the sugar, boil and pot.

Quince

QUINCE
This can possess the most attractive and unique flavour of all. The fruit is short of acid but has ample pectin.

1.8kg (4 lb) quinces (peeled, cored, and either cut into cubes or globes, or grated coarsely), juice of 2 lemons, 2¾kg (6 lb) sugar, 1¾–2¼ litres (3–4 pints) water, according to the ripeness of the fruit.

Simmer slowly until tender (20–35 minutes), add the lemon juice and the sugar, boil and pot.

QUINCE AND APPLE
Only if you want to eke out the quinces!

1kg (2 lb) prepared quinces (see above), 1kg (2 lb) prepared cooking apples, 1.9kg (4¼ lb) sugar, 1 litre (2 pints) water.

Cook the fruit separately (the apples in 300ml/½ pint water and the quince in 900ml/1½ pints water) as the apples will not take so long as the quinces. Mix the two pulps together, add the sugar, boil and pot.

Raspberry

RASPBERRY
This is always known as a standard jam which needs no

additional pectin or acid. 3 lb of raspberries and 3 lb of sugar gives a 5 lb yield.

Recipe 1
1.8kg (4 lb) raspberries, 1.8kg (4 lb) sugar, no water.

Simmer to extract the juice, then add the sugar, boil very quickly. The set is not strong. Do not be late in potting and sealing airtight.

Recipe 2
A better set is obtained if acid and pectin are added like this:

1.8kg (4 lb) raspberries, juice and pith of 3 lemons, 2kg (4½ lb) sugar, no water. (The pith should be placed in a muslin bag and removed after cooking.)

Simmer gently with the lemon until medium soft (15–18 minutes), add the sugar, boil quickly for 3–3½ minutes, pot and seal airtight.

(Home-made pectin can also be used successfully – page 25 – especially if you are making *Seedless Raspberry* jam when the pips are seived out before adding the sugar.)

RASPBERRY AND APPLE
See *Apple and Raspberry* (page 47).

RASPBERRY AND LOGANBERRY
See *Loganberry and Raspberry* (page 52).

RASPBERRY AND RED CURRANT
An easy, foolproof, delicious jam which sets easily.

1kg (2 lb) raspberries, 1kg (2 lb) red currants, 300ml (½ pint) water, 1.9kg (4¼ lb) sugar.

Cook the red currants separately in the water, add the raspberries, simmer, add the sugar, boil and pot.

RASPBERRY AND STRAWBERRY
Use equal weight of each fruit (i.e. 1kg/2 lb each), then follow the method for *Raspberry Recipe 2* (above).

Red Currant

RED CURRANT
1.8kg (4 lb) currants, 300ml (½ pint) water, 2–2½kg (4½–5 lb) sugar.

Cook the currants gently to extract the juice, pass through a sieve to collect up the many seeds, return the pulp to the pan, add the sugar, boil and pot.

White currants are best made into jelly or added to red or black currants. Currants are a rich source of pectin (see page 25).

Rhubarb

RHUBARB

With rhubarb grown in many gardens, this is a cheap jam to make. Does not contain acid or pectin.

2kg (4 lb) rhubarb (peeled or cut into 1cm/½ in pieces), 2kg (4 lb) sugar, pith and juice of 2 lemons, no water. (The pith should be put in a muslin bag and removed after cooking.)

A good set and complementary flavour is obtained by adding pectin in the form of apple, currant or gooseberry juice (page 25).

Cook the rhubarb until soft (not mushy), add the lemon and the sugar, boil and pot.

RHUBARB AND BLACK CURRANT
See *Black Currant and Rhubarb* (page 48).

RHUBARB AND GINGER
Follow the *Rhubarb* recipe above, adding 2 dessertspoonfuls ground ginger during cooking.

RHUBARB AND GOOSEBERRY
See *Gooseberry and Rhubarb* (page 51).

RHUBARB AND ORANGE
Fresh flavour with economy.

1.4kg (3 lb) rhubarb, 450g (1 lb) orange flesh, juice and pith of 4 oranges, no water, 1.7kg (3¾ lb) sugar. (The pith should be in a muslin bag and removed after cooking.)

Simmer the rhubarb carefully with the orange and the pith and peel. Add the sugar, stir well round, boil and pot.

RHUBARB AND RASPBERRY
A good economical jam.

1kg (2 lb) rhubarb, 1kg (2 lb) raspberries or loganberries, 150ml (¼ pint) water, 2kg (4 lb) sugar.

Cook the rhubarb in the water. When soft, add the raspberries or loganberries and continue cooking. Add the sugar, boil and pot.

Strawberry

STRAWBERRY

A delicious fruit, but it's not an easy jam to perfect. Long cooking should be avoided or the fruit will be mashed down and lose colour. It contains no acid or pectin.

2kg (4 lb) strawberries, 2kg (4 lb) sugar, no water, 400ml (½ pint) red currant or gooseberry juice.

Simmer carefully, stir frequently, add the sugar and the fruit juice, boil rapidly to setting. Wait until almost cold before potting to ensure an even distribution of fruit.

STRAWBERRY AND GOOSEBERRY
See *Gooseberry and Strawberry* (page 51).

STRAWBERRY AND RASPBERRY
See *Raspberry and Strawberry* (page 55).

VEGETABLE JAMS
Selected vegetables make attractive, economical and cheap jams. The best varieties are given on pages 43–44.

Beetroot

BEETROOT
This is quite tasty but needs acid, pectin and flavourings.

1.8kg (4 lb) beetroot, 1 litre (2 pints) water, 1.8kg (4 lb) sugar, rind and pith and juice of 4 lemons. (The pith should be in a muslin bag and removed after cooking.)

Wash the beetroot (whole and unskinned) and cook until tender. Pull off the skins and cut the roots into cubes. Put the beetroot back into the pan, bring to simmering, add the sugar, plus the lemon, boil and pot.

As flavouring, add during the final boil 2 teaspoonfuls ground cinnamon or 2 teaspoonfuls vanilla essence.

BEETROOT AND CARROT
As above, using equal weights of each (i.e. 1kg/2 lb) and

cooking separately (the beetroot in 600ml/1 pint of water, and the carrot in just enough water to cover).

Carrot

CARROT
1.8kg (4 lb) young fresh carrots (preferably), water to cover, 1.8kg (4 lb) sugar, rind, pith and juice of 4 lemons. (The pith should be in a muslin bag and removed after cooking.)

Wash and scrape the carrots and cut into 1cm (½ in) cubes. Place in a pan with water to cover and cook until soft but not mushy.

The cubes can now remain as they are or be passed through a sieve to make a pulp. Add the sugar, plus the lemon, boil, pot and seal airtight.

CARROT AND BEETROOT
See *Beetroot and Carrot*, above.

Cucumber

CUCUMBER
1.8kg (4 lb) cucumber, 1.8kg (4 lb) sugar. To each 600ml (1 pint) of juice and pulp, add 12g (½ oz) root ginger and rind, pith and juice of 2 lemons.

Peel and slice the cucumber, place it in a pan with the rind and pith and ginger (in a muslin bag) and cook gently to produce a medium pulp, then add the sugar and the lemon juice, boil and pot *or* weigh, cover with equal weight of sugar and stand for 24 hours. Bring to boil and pot. The seeds can be sieved out.

Marrow

MARROW
This is a soft jam.

1.8kg (4 lb) prepared marrow (in cubes or slices), rind, pith and juice of 4 lemons, 25g (1 oz) bruised dried root ginger, 1.8kg (4 lb) sugar.

Cook the marrow until firm-tender, then drain. Return it to the pan, add the lemon, and the ginger (in a muslin bag), bring to the boil, add the sugar, boil and pot.

MARROW AND GINGER

A very popular and delicious concoction.

1.8kg (4 lb) prepared marrow cubes, 1.8kg (4 lb) sugar, juice of 4 lemons, rind and pith of 4 lemons and 42g (1½ oz) bruised dried root ginger (in a muslin bag) or 3 level teaspoonfuls of ground powder ginger.

Cook the cubes gently so that they are still quite firm; steaming holds their shape best.

Place them in a dish, sprinkle with the sugar and leave for 24 hours; this will result in a substantial amount of liquid.

Return the marrow to the pan, bring to the heat slowly to liquefy the sugar and cook until the cubes take on a yellowish transparent appearance, but do not lose their shape. Setting is best tested by the plate or flake test. Pot hot and seal airtight.

MARROW AND PEAR

More flavoursome than plain pear.

1kg (2 lb) marrow, 1kg (2 lb) pears, 2kg (4 lb) sugar, rind, pith and juice of 3 lemons, 2 level teaspoonfuls ground ginger.

Peel and dice, de-seed the marrow, and steam until firm-tender. Peel, core and cube the pears and cook to soften, not to mash. Add the marrow and pear together, plus the sugar. Add the rind and pith of the lemon and the ground ginger in a muslin bag (which should be removed after cooking) and add the lemon juice. Bring to the boil slowly and pot.

Pumpkin

PUMPKIN

As *Marrow* (page 58), but add sliced orange rind and pith of 2 oranges and 25g (1 oz) bruised root ginger in a muslin bag and add the juice of 2 oranges with the cubes.

PUMPKIN AND ORANGE

As *Marrow* (page 58), but add orange rind, pith (in a muslin bag) and juice of 2 oranges for 1.8kg (4 lb) pumpkin cubes. If bitter oranges are used, the ginger can be omitted.

Tomato

TOMATO

1.8kg (4 lb) prepared tomatoes, 1.8kg (4 lb) sugar, no water, rind and pith of 2 lemons in a muslin bag.

Scald the tomatoes, remove their skins. Cut them in halves. Place them in a pan and cook for a short while (3–5 minutes), sieve out the seeds. Add the sugar (1 teaspoonful of ground ginger can be mixed in) and the lemon, bring to the boil and pot.

TOMATO (GREEN) (Mock Greengage)

As above, but with slightly longer simmering. Cook if possible in a copper or brass pan.

4

FRUIT JELLIES, CONSERVES, BUTTERS AND CHEESES

What is a Jelly?

It is a preserve of fruit and sugar which is clear and colourful and consists of the fruit without its attendant 'pieces' such as pulp, skins, seeds and pips.

A PERFECT JELLY is:

1. Firmly set, able to hold its shape and to quiver when taken from the jar.
2. Brilliantly sparkling in colour.
3. Clear right through, top and bottom.
4. Abounding in the natural fruit flavour.
5. Able to keep well in store.

A BAD JELLY is:

1. Stiff, hard or syrupy and liquid.
2. Dull and unattractive in colour.
3. Partly or wholly cloudy.
4. Lacking flavour, or of a foreign flavour.
5. Unable to store well (mouldy, fermented or crystallized).

THE MOST SUITABLE FRUITS

These possess a most distinct and attractive flavour and colour and have enough acid and pectin to set well: cooking apple, crab apple, bilberry, black currant, blackberry, cranberry, damson, elderberry, gooseberry, greengage, lemon, lime, loganberry, medlar, mulberry, orange, plum, quince, red currant, rowan and sloe.

TRACING MISTAKES

These are fully described in Chapter 2, page 35.

The Practical Programme

Here is the best method for producing successful jelly:

1. Select, prepare and cut up the fruit.
2. Weigh, place into the pan and crush.
3. Add water, little or much.
4. Add acid, if necessary, e.g. for medlar.
5. Simmer to cook and extract the juice.
6. Test for pectin. Add pectin, if necessary, e.g. for elderberry.
7. Strain.
8. Return to the pan, bring to the boil.
9. Add sugar.
10. Boil rapidly.
11. Test for setting.
12. Remove scum.
13. Pot hot to top.
14. Seal airtight.

DETAILED INSTRUCTIONS ON THE ABOVE PROCEDURE

1. There is no need to take currants off the bunch, or hull strawberries, or top and tail gooseberries, as these will be sieved later – what we want is the juice.

2. Weigh the pan and the fruit. Squash down the fruit to break it and help release the juice.

3. Juicy fruits, e.g. blackberries, need 450ml (¾ pint) water per 1.8kg (4 lb); stiff fruits, e.g. apples, need 1–1¾ litres (2–3 pints) water per 1.8kg (4 lb); hard fruits, e.g. quinces, need 2.25–2.8 litres (4–5 pints) water per 1.8kg (4 lb).

4. Add acid – lemon juice or citric or tartaric acid (see page 22).

5. Simmer gently for ¾–1¼ hours to cook the fruit and make sure *all* the juice is extracted.

6. Test for pectin. If low, add lemon pith and rind or pectin-rich fruit, e.g. gooseberry (see page 25).

7. Strain. Pour boiling water through the jelly bag or cloth. Discard the water and allow the fruit pulp to drip through the double layer of butter muslin or linen or felt, overnight

if necessary.

A *second extraction* is possible where fruits are rich in pectin, e.g. red currants. Strain the fruit (as above), for an hour. Return the pulp left behind to the pan, add water to cover (i.e. half the quantity added at first), and simmer for ¾–1 hour. Then pass this through the jelly bag or cloth. The two extracts can then be mixed together.

The strained juice should be tested for pectin quantity and, if deficient, either simmered to draw off some of the water or have added a pectin-rich juice (prepared ready).

8. Measure the volume of juices, return the pan to the boil.
9. Add sugar according to the recipe. If the pectin shows a good clot (see page 24) add 450g (1 lb) sugar to 600ml (1 pint) of juice; if a weak clot add 350g (¾ lb) sugar to 600ml (1 pint).
10. Boil rapidly. The setting point will be reached more quickly than with jam.
11. Test after 10–12 minutes' boiling using the flake test (page 28), supplemented if necessary with a sugar boiling thermometer reading at 104–105°C (200–221°F).
12. Clear the scum off quickly.
13. Pot as quickly as possible in a warm kitchen or near a warm oven: if there is delay or a cold draught, the jelly may start to set in the cooking pan. If the jam pan and jars are allowed to stand on a wooden board, this will help to retain the heat. Pour slowly so that no bubbles are formed. Fill to the top.
14. Cover with a waxed disc and leave to cool before putting on a cellophane dust cover. Or seal with a plastic or twist top (in which case there is no need for a wax disc). Be careful not to tilt the jars during cooling as that will upset the level and spoil the surface. It is not easy to give a ruling as to the weight of jelly produced because of the varied quantities of juice extracted, but it is somewhere around 2¼kg (5 lb) for each 1.4kg (3 lb) of sugar.

Pectin-based Jellies

This is a method where commercially-made pectins are used and the process differs slightly as follows:

1. Wash the fruit.
2. Crush the fruit, add water and simmer to extract the juice.
3. Strain the juice as on page 62.
4. Weigh the juice and sugar separately.
5. Place in the pan.
6. Cook rapidly.
7. Add commercial pectin (powder or liquid); see instructions on packet or bottle.
8. Heat to produce a rolling boil as directed (usually ½–1 minute).
9. Remove from the heat, skim, pot and seal.

About 1.6kg (3½ lb) jelly is made from 1.6kg (3½ lb) fruit and 1.4kg (3 lb) sugar.

A SCORE CARD
See page 45 for details of the points awarded for each quality that a jelly has.

JELLY RECIPES
All the recipes use 1.8kg (4 lb) fruit. Follow the general method on page 62.

Apple
APPLE (CRAB, COOKING OR WINDFALL)
Wash and cut up into medium slices 1.8kg (4 lb) apples, put into a pan with 1.15 litres (2 pints) of water, simmer for 1¼ hours, strain, add 450g (1 lb) sugar to 600ml (1 pint) of juice, boil, test and pot.

To give flavour, the juice of 2 lemons, plus peel coarsely sliced, can be added with the cooking.

APPLE AND QUINCE
See *Quince and Apple* (page 69).

APPLE AND RED CURRANT
See *Red Currant and Apple* (page 70).

Bilberry
BILBERRY
This jelly has good flavour and colour, but needs both acid

and pectin (e.g. apple or gooseberry pectin).

1.8kg (4 lb) fruit, 300ml (½ pint) water, citric acid (1 level teaspoonful), ¾ lb (350g) sugar to each pint of juice.

Black Currant

BLACK CURRANT
A most valuable jelly. 1.8kg (4 lb) washed fruit (on stalks), 1.4 litres (2½ pints) water, 450g (1 lb) sugar for each 600ml (1 pint) of juice. For economy, two extracts can be made using 900ml (1½ pints) water at the first and then 600ml (1 pint) for the second cooking. Follow the recipe for two extracts (page 63).

BLACK CURRANT AND APPLE
1kg (2 lb) currants (on stalks), 1kg (2 lb) cooking apples (cut into slices), 1.15 litres (2 pints) water, 450g (1 lb) sugar for each 600ml (1 pint) of extract. Simmer long to extract both currant and apple juice. This jelly sets well so try it for setting after 8–10 minutes, then pot.

Blackberry

BLACKBERRY (BRAMBLE)
One of the most popular jellies and deservedly so.

1.8kg (4 lb) washed blackberries, 450ml (¾ pint) water, 4 tablespoonfuls lemon juice (to provide the acid if the berries are deficient), 450g (1 lb) sugar to each 600ml (1 pint) of juice.

BLACKBERRY AND APPLE
1.4kg (3 lb) blackberries, 450g (1 lb) cooking apples, 600ml (1 pint) water, no lemon juice, 450g (1 lb) sugar to each 600ml (1 pint) of juice.

Cherry

CHERRY
A delicate but intriguing flavour and colour. Use ripe, red or black cherries (see varieties, page 37).

1.8kg (4 lb) fruit (stoned), 450ml (¾ pint) water, add 4 tablespoonfuls lemon juice plus home-made pectin (e.g. gooseberry). Simmer long to extract what juice is available. Add 450g (1 lb) sugar per 600ml (1 pint) of juice.

Cranberry

CRANBERRY AND APPLE

1kg (2 lb) washed berries, 1kg (2 lb) cooking apples, 1.15 litres (2 pints) water. There is no need to add acid or pectin. It makes a good set and has a nice sharp flavour and colour. Simmer both fruits together. Add 450g (1 lb) sugar to each 600ml (1 pint) juice. Test for setting.

Damson

DAMSON

An easy jelly to make and one that is abounding in flavour. 1.8kg (4 lb) fruit. Two extracts can be made if desired (as for *Black Currant*): 1.15 litres (2 pints) water for the first extract and 600ml (1 pint) water for the second extract. Strain and add both together, add 450g (1 lb) sugar to each 600ml (1 pint) of juice, boil to setting, pot hot.

Elderberry

ELDERBERRY AND APPLE

Cooking apples or crab apples can be used. It is best to add apples to this jelly and not make elderberry jelly on its own as elderberry does not set well.

1kg (2 lb) elderberries (on the stalk), 1kg (2 lb) sliced apples, each cooked separately with just enough water to cover (900ml/ 1½ pints). Strain the juice, mix together, add barely 450g (1 lb) sugar to each 600ml (1 pint) juice, boil, test and pot.

Gooseberry

GOOSEBERRY

1.8kg (4 lb) gooseberries (with tops and tails), 1.15 litres (2 pints) water, 450–550g (1–1¼ lb) sugar to each 600ml (1 pint) of juice. Follow the standard recipe. Two extracts can be taken, in which case use 600ml (1 pint) water in each extract.

The final colour will follow that of the ripe gooseberry (see varieties, page 38).

GOOSEBERRY (MUSCAT)

1.8kg (4 lb) green gooseberries (not fully ripe), 450ml (¾ pint) water. Simmer to extract the juice, strain, add 450g (1 lb) sugar to each 600ml (1 pint) juice, plus 4 elderflower heads immersed in the boiling jelly. It sets easily. Remove the elderflower heads, test and pot as per the standard recipe.

GOOSEBERRY AND RED CURRANT
A good setter. 1kg (2 lb) of each fruit (unstalked), 600ml (1 pint) water or 450ml (¾ pint) if ripe fruit is used. Make separate extracts. Add 450g (1 lb) sugar for each 600ml (1 pint) of juice. Watch out for setting after 7–10 minutes, then pot hot as usual.

GOOSEBERRY AND STRAWBERRY
See *Strawberry and Gooseberry* (page 72).

Japonica

JAPONICA
This is a fast setter although it is well to add 2 tablespoonfuls lemon juice. It makes a nice pink-orange jelly.

1.8kg (4 lb) washed and sliced fruit (mature not hard green), 2.8–3.5 litres (5–6 pints) water. Simmer together long and steady for 1–1¼ hours. Strain, add 450g (1 lb) sugar per 600ml (1 pint) of juice, and pot as usual.

Loganberry

LOGANBERRY
Has a vivid colour and fragrant flavour. Use fully ripe fruit (not over-ripe). To encourage a good set, add 2 tablespoonfuls lemon juice before cooking. Otherwise, simmer 1.8kg (4 lb) berries with 450–600ml (¾–1 pint) water, strain, add 450g (1 lb) sugar per 600ml (1 pint) of juice, boil, test for setting and pot hot.

Mint

MINT (APPLE)
1.8kg (4 lb) sliced apples (green cookers), 1.4 litres (2½ pints) water, the juice of 3 lemons, 4 top tender sprigs of mint (or ½ cup fresh chopped mint leaves in a bag or finely chopped loose). Cook all the ingredients to a pulp, strain, add 450g (1 lb) sugar

to each 600ml (1 pint) of juice, bring to the boil, test for setting and pot. A bright-green edible colour (available from shops) will help give a good appearance.

If an acid flavour is to be produced, then use 900ml (1½ pints) for a preliminary cooking, and just before straining add 600ml (1 pint) white vinegar plus another supply of mint. Bring back to the boil, strain, test and pot.

Orange

ORANGE (AND APPLE)
A pleasant jelly of pronounced and distinct flavour.

5 sweet oranges, 1.4kg (3 lb) cooking or crab apples, 2.3–2.8 litres (4–5 pints) water.

Wash and cut the apples into medium slices. Wash and cut the oranges into slices, but without removing the orange pith. Add the water and simmer gently for 1–1½ hours until tender and the juice is all extracted.

Strain (this may take some while, do not hurry), add 450g (1 lb) sugar per 600ml (1 pint) of juice, boil rapidly for 8–12 minutes to setting, pot and cover.

Plum

PLUM
Wash 1.8kg (4 lb) strongly-flavoured red Victoria or black plums (see varieties, page 39). Simmer in 700ml (1¼ pints) water in which 3 tablespoonfuls lemon juice have been added. Strain, add 450g (1 lb) sugar for each 600ml (1 pint) of juice, boil, pot and cover.

Quince

QUINCE
Perhaps the nicest of all jellies for flavour, colour and consistency. It needs some acid so add 4 tablespoonfuls lemon juice.

Cook 1.8kg (4 lb) ripe quince (washed and cut into small cubes or sliced) with 2.4 litres (4½ pints) water and the lemon juice in a covered pan until mashy and tender (1–1¼ hours) and strain.

Carry out a second extraction using 1.15 litres (2 pints) water. Add both extracts together, stir in 450g (1 lb) sugar to each 600ml (1 pint) of juice, bring up to boiling, test for setting (it should be ready), pot and cover.

QUINCE AND APPLE

The quince and apple are highly complementary and possibly cheaper than quince alone. Cook 1kg (2 lb) of each separately, add them together and continue with the standard recipe.

Raspberry

RASPBERRY

Another popular jelly, good for soothing sore throats if 2 tablespoonfuls white vinegar are added as boiling is finished just before potting.

It is not a good setter and so 4 tablespoonfuls lemon juice should be added, before simmering, to 1.8kg (4 lb) fruit. Hardly any water is used to assist the gentle extraction of juice. It helps to mash down the fruit. Then strain, bring to the boil, add 450g (1 lb) sugar to each 600ml (1 pint) of juice in the pan, and boil hard to setting point.

RASPBERRY AND RED CURRANT
See *Red Currant and Raspberry* (page 70).

Red Currant

RED CURRANT

An excellent jelly either as a confection or as a complement to meat: a good setter and has a delightful colour.

Wash 1.8kg (4 lb) ripe red currants (white currants can be used partly but will lead to a pink jelly) on the stalk, place in the pan with 600ml (1 pint) water and simmer gently until the currants are broken down and mashed. Strain, measure, return to the pan and boil, add 550g (1¼ lb) sugar to each 600ml (1 pint) of juice, boil to jell, pot and cover.

RED CURRANT (CONCENTRATED)

A firmer and stronger-flavoured jelly can be made by not adding any water to the fruit (1.8kg/4 lb). Simmer slowly, strain and drain, add 550g (1¼ lb) sugar to each 600ml (1 pint) of juice, bring to boiling and in 1–1¼ minutes it will be ready to pot and cover. If there is any delay, setting could start in the pan due to the high concentration of acid and pectin.

RED CURRANT AND APPLE
An excellent setter, easy to make and good value.

1.4kg (3 lb) red currants, 450g (1 lb) cooking apples. Simmer separately in 300ml (½ pint) water and 900ml (1½ pints) water respectively. Add them together, bring to the boil, mix in 450g (1 lb) sugar to each 600ml (1 pint) of juice, boil, test, pot and cover.

RED CURRANT AND GOOSEBERRY
See *Gooseberry and Red Currant* (page 67).

RED CURRANT AND RASPBERRY
This has a rather softer flavour than that made with red currants alone.

Follow the standard recipe with equal parts of each fruit (1.8kg/4 lb in total), but cook them separately without acid (no water with the raspberries, 450ml/¾ pint water with the red currants). Simmer slowly, strain the mixed extracts, measure, bring to the boil, add 450g (1 lb) sugar to each 600ml (1 pint) of juice, boil hard and in a few minutes setting will be reached, pot and cover.

RED CURRANT AND RHUBARB
See *Rhubarb and Red Currant* (below).

Rhubarb

RHUBARB AND RED CURRANT (OR BLACK CURRANT)
Rhubarb is not the best for jellies, but it is cheap.

1kg (2 lb) sliced rhubarb (red stalks), 1kg (2 lb) currants (on strigs), 450–600ml (¾–1 pint) water for the black currants, 150ml (¼ pint) water for the red currants or rhubarb.

Simmer separately to extract all the juice available: the black currants will take the longest time, the red currants not so long, and the rhubarb the shortest time. Strain, add together, bring to the boil, add 450g (1 lb) sugar to each 600ml (1 pint) juice, boil, pot and cover.

Rose Hip

ROSE HIP – WITH APPLES

This usually produces a dark red jelly.

You can use equal parts of hips and haws (if so, add 2 tablespoonfuls lemon juice to the hips) or all hips to total 450g (1 lb), 1.4kg (3 lb) crab or cooking apples. Keep the fruit separate. Wash both, add water to cover and simmer separately. Strain and mix together. Bring to the boil and add 450g (1 lb) sugar to each 600ml (1 pint) of juice, boil to setting, pot and cover.

Rowan

ROWAN (MOUNTAIN ASH) – WITH APPLES

It is best to use apples with these berries, as the apples improve and soften the somewhat bitter flavour of the rowan. There will be enough acid and pectin for a good set.

Wash 1kg (2 lb) berries thoroughly (especially if gathered from a tree near a road), and simmer with 900ml–1.15 litres (1½–2 pints) water. Wash and slice 1kg (2 lb) cooking apples and simmer with 600ml (1 pint) of water. Strain and mix both extracts together. Bring to the boil, add 450g (1 lb) sugar to each 600ml (1 pint) of juice, boil rapidly, test for setting, pot and cover.

Sloe

SLOE – WITH APPLES (to soften the flavour)

The set is excellent.

1¼kg (2½ lb) sloes, 675g (1½ lb) cooking or crab apples.

Wash and prick the sloes, slice the apples. Add water to cover: 600ml (1 pint) for the sloes, 300ml (½ pint) for the apples. Simmer separately until tender-soft. Strain, mix together, bring to the boil, add 450g (1 lb) sugar to each 600ml (1 pint) of juice, pot and cover.

Strawberry

STRAWBERRY

Not popular, but it has a 'gentle' flavour.

1.8kg (4 lb) strawberries, 300ml (½ pint) water.

Add 4 tablespoonfuls lemon juice before simmering and add home-made pectin just before potting. Follow the standard method and add 450g (1 lb) sugar to each 600ml (1 pint) of juice.

STRAWBERRY AND GOOSEBERRY (OR RED CURRANT)
Gooseberries (or red currants) are added to give a satisfactory set.

Simmer 1kg (2 lb) of each fruit separately in water: 150ml (¼ pint) water for the strawberries; 300ml (½ pint) water for the gooseberries; and a mere trace for the red currants. Strain, mix, bring to the boil, add 450g (1 lb) sugar to each 600ml (1 pint), boil test, pot and cover.

CONSERVES

This is a 'whole' fruit jam where the fruit is whole or halved and maintains its original shape, being permeated with sugar and suspended in a jelly or syrup of high sugar concentration – perhaps the most delicious of sugar-fruit confections.

There are two variations:

1. Where the fruit is treated with sugar prior to boiling; and
2. Where the fruit is boiled in a syrup. This is sometimes known as a 'preserve'.

The Dry Sugar Method

For dry sugaring, the most suitable fruits and vegetables are: apple, loganberry, marrow, melon, pear, quince, raspberry, rhubarb and strawberry.

PROGRAMME
1. Select and prepare the fruit fully (as for normal cooking).
2. Place the fruit in an appropriate container between layers of sugar (usually 450g/1 lb sugar to each 450g/1 lb fruit).
3. Leave for 24 hours to allow the fruit juice to be extracted and the fruit itself to toughen.
4. Place in the preserving pan (with any extras, such as colour, flavouring or acid).
5. Bring to the boil, which will be complete (a) when there is a set (jell), or (b) when the syrup is thick. In both cases, the fruit should be a firm entity, either whole or part.

6. Allow to cool off slightly so that when potted the fruit will remain evenly suspended.
7. Seal airtight.

Specific Recipes
1.8kg (4 lb) sugar to 1.8kg (4 lb) fruit is used in the following recipes, unless otherwise stated.

APPLE
Cut the apple into cubes. Put the cubes into a boiling syrup consisting of 1.8kg (4 lb) sugar in 900ml (1½ pints) water. Flavour with 100g (4 oz) bruised root ginger placed in a muslin bag and removed after cooking. Boil for 40–60 minutes when the cubes will become clear yellow.

CHERRY
Use whole or halved, stoned red cherries (May Duke, Morello or Flemish Red), 1.6kg (3½ lb) sugar, plus the white pith and peel of 2 lemons (placed in a muslin bag which is removed after cooking).

MARROW
Use ripe and firm marrow. Cut into 1cm (½ in) cubes. Flavour with ginger as in the *Apple* recipe above. Use 1.6kg (3½ lb) sugar.

MELON
Makes a delicious conserve. Choose ripe and firm melon. Any colour may be used but deep orange looks most attractive. Cut it into 1cm (½ in) cubes, and add ginger (as in the *Apple* recipe above) and the white pith of 2 lemons (both in a muslin bag which is removed after cooking).

PEAR
Another delicious one. Pink colouring may be added or a variety of pear which goes pink on cooking may be used.

Firm ripe dessert pears are cubed or sliced and then sugared, but hard cooking pears must be cooked firm first. Add ginger and the pith of 2 lemons in a muslin bag which should be removed after cooking.

PINEAPPLE
Cut into chunks and use the white pith.

QUINCE
Cut into cubes and cook firm, then sugar, using some of the cooking liquid as desired.

RASPBERRY
The fruit should be firm-ripe and evenly-coloured. Add the pith of 2 lemons in a muslin bag which should be removed after cooking.

RHUBARB
Choose an early red variety. Use 1.6kg (3½ lb) sugar. Add white lemon pith (in a muslin bag which should be removed after cooking) and red colouring (if liked).

STRAWBERRY
Sugar, then boil for 3–4 minutes. Put into a basin for 8 hours and then boil again to reach setting or a thick consistency. Add the white pith of 2 lemons in a muslin bag (which should be removed after cooking).

The Boiling Syrup Method: (a) Rapid; (b) Slow
The best fruits and vegetables are apple, apricot, blackberry, cherry, fig, grapefruit, loganberry, marrow, melon, nectarine, peach, pear, pineapple, plum, quince, raspberry and straw-berry.

(a) THE RAPID METHOD
1. Select, prepare and cut the fruit into cubes or slices.
2. Place the fruit into boiling syrup, 450g (1 lb) sugar to each 600ml (1 pint) water, and continue to boil.
3. Test with a jam thermometer. It should be 103–104°C (218–220°F).
4. Take off the heat and allow to cool for 15 minutes to plump up the fruit, stirring occasionally.
5. Bring to the boil.
6. Allow to cool down to form a skin.
7. Stir to ensure even distribution of the fruit.
8. Pot into hot jars.
9. Seal airtight.

(b) THE SLOW METHOD

This gives superior fruit quality as the sugar is made to diffuse into the fruit cells.

1. Select and prepare the fruit.
2. Boil the fruit in a weak syrup, 550g (1¼ lb) sugar to 1.15 litres (2 pints) water, just to cover, until firm-tender but not squashed. (This is known as the First Boil.)
3. Remove from the heat and stand aside for 24 hours. Cool quickly.
4. Increase the sugar concentration by adding 300g/11 oz.
5. Boil for 2 minutes (the Second Boil).
6. Stand aside again for 24 hours. Cool quickly.
7. Increase the sugar concentration by adding 460g/17 oz.
8. Boil for 2 minutes (the Third and Final Boil).
9. Remove from the heat and cool to form a skin.
10. Stir to distribute the fruit evenly.
11. Pot into hot jars.
12. Seal airtight.

The result is a fine quality conserve with the fruit plump, brilliant in colour and of a fresh fruit flavour.

Acid, flavour and colour may be added as desired. Over-boiling must be avoided or the colour may be darkened and crystallization occur while in storage.

SPECIAL HINTS

Berried Fruits
These require two boilings only, but add the third step sugar (no. 7 above) at the second step (no. 4 above).

Medium-firm Fruits
For peaches, plums and figs, follow the standard method. Prick plums to avoid bursting.

Hard Fruits
Apples, pears and quinces may need cooking in plain water first until firm-tender followed by cooking in the sugar syrup.

Syrup
If the level falls considerably, add boiling water (not syrup) up to the original level.

If there is too much syrup, use it for other cooking, but make sure the fruit in the jars is covered with the syrup.

FRUIT BUTTERS

This is a delicious fruit preserve. It is a concentrated smooth paste which, though stiff, spreads easily, its chief attribute being that it is free from skins, pips and seeds. It is all fruit pulp and sugar, and this is most appreciated by those whose digestion may be upset by eating skins, etc., and also, for those whose dentures are not a too perfect fit!

The operation is simple and foolproof:

1. Wash ripe, sound fruit. Cut up large fruit such as apples and pears, but there is no need for strigging, topping and tailing, etc.
2. Weigh the pan (and the spoon).
3. Put the fruit into the pan and add sufficient water to cover.
4. Add acid if necessary (see pages 22 and 77).
5. Simmer slowly until the fruit is soft.
6. Pass through a plastic, nylon or hair sieve (not a metal one) to exclude all but the pulp.
7. Return to the pan and weigh. Work out the weight of the pulp.
8. To each 450g (1 lb) of pulp add 225–350g (½–¾ lb) sugar. Stir well to dissolve the sugar.
9. Return the pan to the heat and stir the sugar in.
10. Boil (not too fierce) for ½–1 hour until the butter is semi-solid, neither runny nor stiff. It must be 'spreadable' *when cold*.
11. Stir frequently or the thick mass may burn at the bottom.
12. Add any flavouring or colour and stir well in.
13. Ladle it hot into hot jars.
14. Seal down hot airtight.

The most suitable fruits for both butter and cheese recipes (see page 78) are: apple, crab apple, apricot, black currant, blackberry, cranberry, damson, gooseberry, grape, loganberry, marrow, medlar, mulberry, peach, pear, plum, quince, rhubarb and tomato.

Fig. 8.   Excluding all but the pulp.
Pressing the fruit pulp through a sieve to remove the large pieces (pips, skins, stalks, etc.) for making fruit butter, fruit cheese or jelly.

ADDING ACID

It does help if the juice of 2 lemons (or ½ teacup of citric or tartaric acid solution) is added at the commencement to each 1.8kg (4 lb) fruit. See also page 22.

FLAVOURS

These, to suit the particular fruit, may be:

apple	– ginger, nutmeg, cinammon, cloves
marrow	– raspberry, strawberry, vanilla, orange
melon	– ginger
pear	– ginger, clove
rhubarb	– lemon, orange, raisin (stoned), damson.

The other fruits are not much improved, but flavour can be included according to personal taste.

SUGAR

White sugar can be used if the pulp has a natural attractive colour or is to be coloured; brown sugar can be used to give partly its own colour and flavour.

FINISHING POINT

This is determined by consistency *not* by the setting point (which is not tested), realizing that the preserve will be thicker when set (cold) than when boiling (hot).

FRUIT CHEESES

The same fruits as recommended for fruit butter are most satisfactory.

This follows the operation for making a fruit butter with the difference that 350–450g (¾–1 lb) sugar is added to each 450g (1 lb) of pulp, and boiling is continued until the pulp is almost solid. The addition of acid as for butters is advised. There is no test for setting.

It is then packed into small, wide-mouth jars or into moulds; rolled and cut into shape; sprinkled with castor sugar, cut into bars and coated with chocolate; used as a filling for chocolates and sweets.

It is delicious when served with game, poultry and other meats.

FRUIT PASTES

This is a cheese which has been dried to the consistency of almond paste and cut into bars, fingers, stars, circles, cubes, etc. It needs no jar, but is stored, wrapped in confectionery paper or foil in tins or boxes sealed with sellotape. Drying is carried out in a very slow oven and the cheese is frequently inspected.

5

MARMALADES AND CURDS

MARMALADES

A MARMALADE is a jam, jelly, thick syrup or pulp in which are suspended slices of fruit or peel. It is made from:

1. Citrus fruits, i.e. oranges, tangerines, lemons, limes, grapefruits, solo or in combination, and;
2. Non-citrus fruits, i.e. apples, apricots, peaches, pears and quinces.

Citrus Fruits
The Standard Operation
The operation is much the same as for the making of jam, but longer cooking is needed to soften the peel. There is a wide choice of marmalades – thick, jelly, shredded and chunky.

Here is the operation:

1. In detergent wash the fruit to get rid of the wax coating. Rinse very thoroughly.
2. Take off the peel.
3. Squeeze out the juice, scoop out the fruit pulp. Shred the peel thinly or thickly: the thinner it is, the quicker the pectin will be released. Slicing is best done by hand with a very sharp knife. Place in a cooking pan. Put the pips into a muslin bag and add to the pan.
4. In a chunky marmalade, the white pith will remain adhering to the peel, but in a jelly one, the pith is better removed and placed in a muslin bag along with the pectin-rich pips during cooking.
5. Add water, usually 2–2¼ litres (3½–4 pints) for each 1kg (2 lb) of fruit, or proportionally (see recipes).

6. Add acid to ensure a good set in the form of lemon juice (juice of 2 lemons), or 1 tablespoonful tartaric or citric acid per 1kg (2 lb) fruit.
7. Cook the fruit with the acid to soften both the fruit and the *peel*. This may take 1½–3 hours (see recipes). It is important to cook the peel before sugar is added. Cooking usually reduces the volume of liquid by half. Remove the muslin bag from the pan.
8. Add sugar, usually 675g–1kg (1½–2 lb) per 450g (1 lb) of fruit (see recipes), i.e. 1.4–1.8kg (3–4 lb) sugar per 1kg (2 lb) of fruit.
9. If the fruit and peel have been fully cooked, the final boiling with the sugar will not take longer than 15–25 minutes.
10. Test for setting (see page 28).
11. The scum can be a nuisance, so skim the surface before boiling ceases. A knob of butter or small quantity of oil placed on the surface will reduce the scum.
12. Allow to cool down until a skin is seen to be developing, then stir round slowly.
13. Pour into warm jars, put on a waxed circle or a twist or plastic top, leave to cool.
14. Fix cellophane or parchment top over the waxed circle.

PRESSURE COOKER COOKING

In order to reduce the rather long cooking time of 1½–3 hours in an open pan, the softening can be achieved in an ordinary pressure cooker, although not so much fruit can be cooked at one time.

600–700ml (1–1¼ pints) water to each 450g (1 lb) fruit is satisfactory. With the fruit and acid, usually 2kg (4½ lb) of fruit and 2 litres (3½ pints) of water can be put in without the rack. Pressure cooking at 7kg (15 lb) for 15–20 minutes is required; after this time the pressure cooker is removed from the source of the heat and the pressure is allowed to reduce at room temperature for 10–15 minutes, when the vent is opened and the lid removed.

The fruit is then treated as per the recipe (pith, pips, peel, etc.) and either boiled with the sugar in the pressure cooker (open) or in an ordinary jam pan up to setting, skimming, cooling, straining and potting.

The above instructions are guidelines only, *always consult the manufacturer's instruction book*.

Recipes for Thick Marmalades

The following are recipes for *thick* marmalades which contain peel, pith, flesh but not pips.

SEVILLE ORANGE

A popular breakfast marmalade which produces a lovely, fruity-flavoured preserve.

1kg (2 lb) Seville oranges, juice of 2 lemons, 2¼ litres (4 pints) water, 1.8kg (4 lb) sugar or proportionately. Follow the standard method. Cook for 1½–1¾ hours.

CHUNKY

1kg (2 lb) Seville oranges, juice of 2 lemons, 1¾–2 litres (3–3½ pints) water, 1.8kg (4 lb) sugar (half can be brown sugar plus 1 tablespoonful of dark treacle).

Cut the peel into small chunks and leave the pith intact. Add the lemon juice and cook for 1¾–2 hours until softened. Pass the pulp through a fine sieve, add the sugar, boil to setting, skim, cool, stir and pot hot, cover when cold.

LEMON

1kg (2 lb) lemons, 2–2¼ litres (3½–4 pints) water, 1.8kg (4 lb) sugar. Limes can be used in place of lemons, giving a pale, crisp-flavoured product.

Follow the standard method.

GRAPEFRUIT

1kg (2 lb) grapefruit, 225g (½ lb) lemons, 3 litres (5½ pints) water, 1.8kg (4 lb) sugar.

Cut the peel medium. Leave in the pith. Put the pips in a muslin bag. Cook for 2 hours until the peel is tender and the volume is reduced by about half. Take out the bag of pips, squeeze well, add the sugar, stir to dissolve, boil fairly rapidly to setting point, half cool, stir, pot and cover when cold.

OLD ENGLISH

1kg (2 lb) Seville oranges, 225g (½ lb) lemons, 2¼ litres (4 pints) water, 1.9kg (4¼ lb) sugar (of which 450g/1 lb brown sugar).

Cut the peel chunky. Put the pith and pips in a muslin bag. Cook for 1½–1¾ hours to reduce the volume by half. Remove the muslin bag. Add the sugar, boil quickly to setting and complete as the standard method.

THREE FRUIT

A good combination is 2 sweet oranges, 2 grapefruit and 3 lemons to a weight of about 1¼kg (2½ lb), 2.5–2.8 litres (4½–5 pints) water, 2¼ kg (5 lb) sugar, not too much pith attached to the peel.

Cook slowly for 1½ hours, add sugar and continue with the standard method.

FOUR FRUIT

The best flavour is obtained from 2 sweet oranges, 1 grapefruit, 2 lemons and 2 cooking apples. But any combination of these fruits can be used without upsetting the result.

Wash and slice the peel of the citrus fruits, cover with water and cook for 12–15 minutes.

Peel and core the apples and cut them into half slices. Press out the citrus juice and cut up the fleshy part.

Add these together and simmer for 15–20 minutes, then add 2kg (4½ lb) sugar and boil to setting. Continue with the standard method.

ORANGE AND LEMON

3 lemons, 3 oranges, 2.8 litres (5 pints) water, 1.8kg (4 lb) sugar. Follow the standard method, prepare, simmer and boil all together.

SEVILLE AND SWEET

A thicker marmalade made from 4 Seville oranges, 2 sweet oranges, 2¼ litres (4 pints) water, 1.8kg (4 lb) sugar, 4 tablespoonfuls lemon juice. Cook all together and follow the recipe for *Chunky Marmalade* (opposite).

Recipes for Jelly Marmalades

These differ from the thick marmalades in that they consist of a clear jelly in which thinly sliced peel is evenly suspended.

SEVILLE ORANGE JELLY

1¼kg (2½ lb) Seville oranges, juice of 2 lemons, 2¼ litres (4 pints) water, 1.6kg (3½ lb) sugar.

The operation is in two parts: (1) to produce the firm sliced peel; and (2) to provide the clear jelly.

Scald the oranges, cut off the peel and the thick pith and slice the peel almost like matchsticks – even in length and size. Cook with 600ml (1 pint) water for 1½–2 hours until tender and firm.

Cut up the fleshy parts and the pith. Put this and the lemon juice, with the pips in a muslin bag, in 1.4 litres (2½ pints) water and cook slowly for 1¾–2 hours.

Pour the liquid from the sliced peel, add to the fleshy pulp and pass through a fine sieve and a jelly bag. This will take about 15–20 minutes.

Put the pulp back into the pan with 600ml (1 pint) water, cook for 15–20 minutes and strain.

Put all the strained juice into the pan and bring to the boil. Add 1.6kg (3½ lb) sugar, allow it to dissolve, add the cooked shredded peel and boil hard to setting. Complete by following the standard method.

GRAPEFRUIT JELLY

This is a rewarding jelly of 'clean' flavour.

Follow the above recipe using two 350g (¾ lb) grapefruit and 3 lemons to a total weight of 1kg–1.1kg (2–2¼ lb). For simmering, about 2.4–2.5 litres (4¼–4½ pints) water will be necessary and 1.4kg (3 lb) sugar. Be sure to strain well to produce a clear jelly.

TANGERINE JELLY

For the most delightful results and satisfactory setting, tangerines should be used to make a jelly (rather than a marmalade) with the addition of lemons and grapefruit, e.g. 1kg (2 lb) tangerines, 2 lemons and 1 grapefruit, to a total weight of 1.3–1.4kg (2¾–3 lb).

Follow the *Seville Orange Jelly* recipe (page 83), but allow only tangerine shreds in the final product. The peel, pith and pips of the grapefruit and lemons are placed in a muslin bag during the simmering, but the pulp of these is added with the tangerine pulp and the tangerine shreds.

TOMATO MARMALADE

Quite economical and tasteful.

5 ripe tomatoes, 4 lemons, 300–450ml (½–¾ pint) water,

1.9kg (4¼ lb) sugar.

Take off the tomato skins by blanching them (putting them into boiling water and then cold water), slice them and put into a china bowl. Extract the lemon juice and add this to the tomato pulp. Slice the lemon peel and put it in a muslin bag with the pith and pips. Add the sugar to the water, dissolve and bring to boiling. Put in the tomato slices and the muslin bag and boil to setting, up to 25–35 minutes.

If shreds are required, cook the sliced lemon peel separately to tender and then add to the boiled tomato pulp just before potting.

RHUBARB MARMALADE

1.6kg (3½ lb) cubed rhubarb, 4 lemons, 990ml (1¾ pints) water, 1½kg (3¼ lb) sugar.

Extract the lemon juice and cook the (sliced) lemon peel in it and the water, with the pips and pith in a muslin bag, until tender. Add the rhubarb cubes and cook carefully until firm-soft. Take out the bag and squeeze it well. Put in the sugar so that it dissolves and return to the heat and boil to setting.

GINGER MARMALADE

This flavour can be added to marmalade by mixing in 13–19g (½–¾ oz) ground ginger or 50g (2 oz) finely chopped fresh root ginger to 1.4kg (3 lb) fruit just prior to the final boiling.

SUGAR-LESS MARMALADE (FOR DIABETICS)

For long keeping this should be potted into metal-capped airtight jars and then sterilized to 80°C (175°F) – see page 113.

3 Seville oranges, 3 lemons, 700ml (1¼ pints) water, 10 saccharine tablets (or an approved powder as per directions), 13g (½ oz) gelatine to each 450g (1 lb) of pulp.

Remove the peel (plus the pith) from the fruit and slice it. Put it into a pan with the pulp, water and saccharine, and with the pips (in a muslin bag). Cook for 30–35 minutes until tender.

Add the gelatine dissolved in ½ cupful of the warm juice. Pot, cover and sterilize if required to keep long.

CITRUS MARMALADE WITH PECTIN BASE

Either home-made apple pectin (page 25) or commercial pectin can be used.

The simple steps are:

1. Wash, peel and shred 1.4kg (3 lb) fruit.
2. Place the peel in a pan with 600ml (1 pint) water.
3. Cook for 10 minutes.
4. Add the juice and the pulp to the cooked peel.
5. Cook for 20 minutes.
6. Add 2.4kg (5¼ lb) sugar to the 1.4kg (3 lb) prepared fruit in the pan.
7. Boil for 5 minutes.
8. Remove from the heat and stir in the pectin.
9. Allow to cook and stir to distribute the shreds.
10. Pot and seal airtight.

This will yield 3.4–3.5kg (7¾–8 lb).

Marmalade from Non-citrus Fruits

This is really a conserve except that the fruit is sliced and the syrup is strained; delicious.

Suitable fruits are apples, apricots, peaches, pears, quinces. Carrots are a suitable vegetable.

Here is the complete and easy operation:

1. Select, prepare and slice the fruit.
2. Place the fruit in a basin with a layer of sugar (450g/1 lb sugar to each 450g/1 lb of fruit).
3. Leave for 24 hours for extraction and hardening.
4. Place the fruit in a pan and bring to boiling and setting point. (Apple slices can be cooked in a muslin bag to stop them breaking down.)
5. Strain the liquid through a jelly bag.
6. Put the strained juice in the pan and add the fruit slices.
7. Bring to the boil and skim.
8. Allow to cool to form a skin.
9. Stir to distribute the slices.
10. Pot and seal airtight.

The precise sugar, lemon juice or acid quantities for some different fruits are shown under Conserves on page 73. Each 1.8kg (4 lb) of the fruit/vegetable listed below requires the following amounts of citric or tartaric acid:

apricots:　½ teaspoonful;
peaches:　1 teaspoonful;
carrots:　2 teaspoonfuls.

A SCORE CARD FOR MARMALADE

The same points which are awarded when judging jams (page 45) are given when judging marmalades.

FRUIT CURDS

These are not true preserves as they contain eggs, butter and sugar, with the fruit. They are highly nutritious, have fine tonic properties and can be used as a jam or in other culinary practices. The quantity of sugar is variable according to the desired sweetness or briskness of the curd. It is important to cook them slowly in order to avoid any risk of curdling. Remember that a curd when cold is much thicker than one which is hot.

Do not serve curds to babies, pregnant women or the elderly as these groups of people may be susceptible to any bacteria in the eggs not destroyed by the cooking process. Make sure you only use the freshest eggs available. Thoroughly wash the shells before breaking them, and be careful not to drop any bits of shell into the egg.

Store the potted curd in a refrigerator and eat within 2–3 weeks.

APPLE CURD

Although not a good keeper, this curd is useful for filling cakes, tarts, etc. Wash, peel, core and slice 1kg (2 lb) cooking apples and simmer slowly in water to cover until fully cooked, when they are mashed to a pulp. Add 450g (1 lb) sugar, a level teaspoonful of ground cinnamon, 2 beaten egg yolks and 75g (3 oz) butter. Place over a moderate heat (do not boil), and stir until the curd is moderately thick. Pot hot and cover with a wax disc. When *cold*, cover with a cellophane top and store in the refrigerator. Eat within 2–3 weeks.

APRICOT CURD

Rather expensive but delicious. Cook 450g (1 lb) fruit (with only enough water to stop it burning) until soft and pass the pulp through a sieve. Place this in a double saucepan with 350–400g (12–14 oz) sugar (stirred to dissolve), the grated rind and juice of 2 lemons, 100g (4 oz) butter and 4 beaten eggs. Heat, stir until moderately thick, pot and cover as with *Apple Curd* above.

GOOSEBERRY CURD

This is made following the method used for *Apple Curd* above. The gooseberries should be green. Simmer 1kg (2 lb) gooseberries with 300ml (½ pint) water. Add 3 eggs (lightly beaten), 75g (3 oz) butter and 450g (1 lb) sugar.

LEMON CURD

This is a recipe which originated many years ago and now seems to be accepted as the standard one. Use 4 eggs, 4 lemons, 100g (4 oz) butter and 450g (1 lb) sugar. Wash the lemons in detergent and rinse thoroughly before use.

Place the butter, eggs, the finely grated rind and juice of the lemons, and the sugar in a double saucepan or in a basin over water. Gently heat (do not boil) and stir to melt the sugar for about 20–25 minutes until it becomes thick. Then pour into hot jars, add waxed circles, allow to cool and then cover and store in a dry, cold place.

LEMON AND APPLE CURD

Follow the recipe for *Apple Curd*, adding the juice and shredded rind of 2 lemons.

MARROW (OR PUMPKIN) CURD

Peel and cut up the marrow to produce 450g (1 lb) cubes, simmer until tender and discard the liquid. Extract the juice of 3 lemons and grate the rind finely. (Make sure you wash the lemons in detergent and rinse them thoroughly before use.) Place in a double saucepan with 350–400g (12–14 oz) sugar and 100g (4 oz) butter. Simmer and stir until medium-thick, remembering that a curd when cold is much thicker than one which is hot. Pot and seal.

ORANGE CURD

4 eggs, 100g (4 oz) butter, 300–400g (10–14 oz) sugar, 3 oranges and 1 lemon. Follow the *Lemon Curd* recipe.

PART TWO

PICKLES
CHUTNEYS,
SAUCES
AND KETCHUPS

6

PICKLES

The high price of vegetables and of commercial pickles and chutneys makes it well worthwhile to produce one's own at home. Home processing is neither difficult nor costly, and the resultant product is certainly equal to, or, more often, superior to that made by a commercial firm.

Equipment

Most of it will already be available in the kitchen. The *preserving pan* or saucepan must not be of brass, copper or iron because of interaction and the subsequent unpleasant taste, but of stainless steel or aluminium or unchipped enamel.

Basins for brining can be of the same materials as those recommended for the pan and also of earthenware, plastic (provided that it is not affected by acid, etc.) or glass.

The *sieve* must be of hair, nylon or plastic, not of metal. Butter muslin over a glass tun-dish or funnel is excellent.

Stirring spoons are best of plastic, wood or glass.

Scales should weigh in grams or quarter ounces.

There is a wide choice of *bottles* and those made specially for vinegar-preserved products are recommended because they are so made and capped that there is no action of the vinegar on the metal. These have metal or plastic caps, screw-down or clip-on, with a lining impervious to the action of vinegar.

Other useful covers are:

1. A bung cork to fit the glass jam-jar or other jar pushed down onto a sheet of stout greaseproof paper or ceresin, with another sheet at the top tied firmly with thin string;
2. A 'bottling' jar which has a glass cap, screw band and spring clip;

3.   A cover of greaseproof, plus wax-coated muslin, tied securely;

4.   Special preserving skin tied on tightly.

Whatever is used (and the special jars are far the best and safest), there must be neither chance of corrosion nor of evaporation; in the former case, the metal is gradually destroyed, and in the latter, the product loses its edible value and becomes hard and distasteful.

The Salt

The *salting or brining* of vegetables is for the purpose of extracting some of the water and carbohydrates from the tissues, making the pickles crisp and preventing the development of bacteria – all with the aim of ensuring successful preservation in store.

Block salt scraped to a powder is still preferred by many, but the fine packet salt is considered a time-saver. The sort which contains chemicals to stop caking may lead to the forming of a slight deposit or the clouding of the vinegar – a bad feature if the jar is to be exhibited.

The *standard brine* can be in *solution* (450g/1 lb salt to 4½ litres/1 gallon water or 2 heaped tablespoonfuls salt to 600ml/ 1 pint water) or in a *dry powdered* form sprinkled between the layers of the prepared vegetables, usually 1 level tablespoonful to 450g (1 lb) vegetables.

Home-made pickles are of a brighter colour and more attractive in flavour than those made commercially because the latter are held in store (until the processors are ready) in a brine for maybe 6–9 months when they are 'cured', becoming dark in colour, transparent and soft. This long curing is neither necessary nor advisable from a home point-of-view.

The Vinegars

BOTTLED VINEGAR

This is usually sold under the name of the manufacturer or bottler, is dependable and contains a minimum of 5–6% acetic acid. For good preservation, the vinegar strength in the final pickle should be at least 3.5% if it is to keep long and well.

DRAUGHT VINEGAR (FROM A BARREL)

Can be good or inferior but may have no more than 3% acid so that the final acid content is no more than 2% which will not keep the pickles well and will probably allow mould or fermentation.

BULK VINEGAR

Usually low in price and useful for cooking or short-time preservation but it may have a low acid content and thus poor preservation power and so could lead to a cloudy covering liquid in the finished pickle.

MALT VINEGAR

Is brown, shining clear and made by the alcoholic fermentation of a malt infusion. It is most popular for pickling as it ensures an attractive flavour and a pleasing colour. The depth of colour in no way determines the quality or percentage of acid.

WINE VINEGAR

Is usually made from inferior wines (alcohol to acetic acid) or from grape juice (sugar to alcohol to acetic acid). It is colourless, delicate of flavour, of top strength and is particularly valuable to use with colourful pickles for show purposes.

SPIRIT VINEGAR

This is distilled from potatoes, grain or starchy vegetables or from yeast liquor, and is of 5% or more acetic acid. Although of high-class quality it has no special advantage over other malt or white wine vinegar.

CIDER VINEGAR

This is much used in the USA and is the conversion of apple wine (alcohol) into acetic acid. It can be obtained at good shops and is not difficult to make at home.

FRUIT VINEGAR

Again, can be an excellent home-made product – usually carrying at least 5% acid which is obtained if the sugar content (determined by a hydrometer) of the fruit juice is at least 12.5. When home-made wine has 'gone off' or 'sour', it can often be converted into quite good vinegar by adding 600ml (1 pint) good vinegar to 2¼ litres (4 pints) of wine, stirring round and leaving exposed to the air, but covered to keep dust out. Keep at 21–23°C (70–75°F) and do not destroy the film of 'mother vinegar' at the top. After 12 weeks or more, the conversion should be complete.

Honey, below standard, can also be used.

WHITE OR BROWN?
Generally, brown malt should be used for top flavour; white wine or white malt for coloured products and for exhibition work.

COLD OR HOT?
The choice is a personal one, as the keeping qualities are not influenced one way or the other. 'Cold' can be used where the attraction of the pickle lies in its crispness (e.g. cabbage or cauliflower) and 'hot' can be used for soft vegetables (e.g. beetroot, cucumber or walnut). 'Hot' means bringing the vinegar up to simmering and pouring in hot (having earlier warmed the jars to prevent cracking).

NON-BREWED
This is a solution of acetic acid, coloured and flavoured, has a sharp taste but does not produce that well-known and well-appreciated pickle obtained by using one of the fermented vinegars.

Spiced Vinegar
The age-old plan of putting whole (pickling) spices in with the pickles is not favoured because the flavour is uneven; nor is the use of powdered spices recommended because they dull the clarity of the pickle and often leave a deposit at the bottom of the jar. It is much easier to pour onto the vegetables a specially-made 'spiced' vinegar.

THE SLOW METHOD
If the 'spiced vinegar' can be made early in the season and kept as wanted, so much the better for flavour. Make it by putting the spice mixture into cold vinegar in a closed jar or bottle and leave it, with occasional shaking or stirring up, for at least 8 weeks.

THE QUICK METHOD
The most usual method for a quick result is to extract the flavour of the spices by steeping them in hot vinegar following

this method:

Place 40–70g (1½–2½ oz) mixed spice in a muslin bag in the top half of a double saucepan along with 1.15 litres (2 pints) vinegar and bring the water in the bottom half of the saucepan up to boiling point, keeping the lid on all the time. But make sure the vinegar does *not boil*.

Alternatively, a large pan of water, over which is placed a china bowl containing the vinegar and the spices (in a muslin bag) can be used if a double saucepan is not available. A china plate is used to cover the vinegar.

The saucepan is then taken off the heat and the spices in the muslin bag in the china bowl or double cooker are allowed to infuse in the hot vinegar for 2½ hours by which time the spicy flavours will have been absorbed by the vinegar.

If the vinegar produced is cloudy, strain through a jelly bag. Then, bottle and label indicating the type of spiced vinegar, e.g. universal, hot, sweet, and so on.

RECIPES FOR MAKING THE SPICE

These vary considerably. They can be bought ready-mixed from shops or made up as liked, perhaps from one of the choices given below:

Ministry of Agriculture Spice Recipe
7g (¼ oz) cinnamon
7g (¼ oz) cloves
7g (¼ oz) mace
7g (¼ oz) whole pimento (allspice)
6 peppercorns

'Grange' Spice Recipe
7g (¼ oz) cinnamon
7g (¼ oz) cloves
7g (¼ oz) white peppercorns
7g (¼ oz) ginger
7g (¼ oz) mace
7g (¼ oz) pimento (allspice)

Sarsons Hot Spice Recipe
28g (1 oz) mustard seed
7g (¼ oz) chillies
14g (½ oz) cloves

14g (½ oz) black peppercorns
28g (1 oz) pimento (allspice)

Special Vinegars

Some recipes advise the use of special vinegars which can be purchased at speciality shops ready-prepared or made at home by steeping the leaves, petals, flowers, roots, etc. in vinegar for 1–6 weeks. The vinegar is then strained, bottled, closely corked and stored in a dark place.

Below are recipes for some special vinegars, using 1.15 litres (2 pints) vinegar.

CELERY
1.15 litres (2 pints) fine, chopped celery – steeped in vinegar for 2 weeks.

CHILLI
100 chilli – steeped in vinegar for 6 weeks.

CUCUMBER
10 small cucumber, 3 onions – steeped in vinegar for 1 week.

HERB
75g (3 oz) any herb – steeped in vinegar for 3 weeks.

HORSERADISH
75g (3 oz) horseradish, 28g (1 oz) shallots – steeped in vinegar for 1 week.

MINT
Pack mint to fill a 1.15 litre (2 pint) jar – steeped in vinegar for 3 weeks.

ONION
½ cupful chopped onion – steeped in vinegar for 2 weeks.

ROSE PETAL
1.15 litres (2 pints) rose petals pressed down – steeped in vinegar for 3 weeks.

TARRAGON
100g (4 oz) tarragon leaves – steeped in vinegar for 3 weeks.

VIOLET
1.15 litres (2 pints) flowers pressed down – steeped in vinegar for 1 week.

What is a Good Pickle?

COVER: No rust or discoloration; must have an acid-proof disc of cork, card, ceresin or plastic.

LABEL AND DATE: This is important. It must include the name, date and any useful short details.

CLEAN JAR: Smears and dirt on the outside indicate carelessness – probably inside as well as outside!

GRADING: Each piece of vegetable/fruit must be of the same size and shape.

COLOUR: Brilliancy is an attractive feature and leads to anticipation of a good pickle.

PACKING: Fill the jar by placing the pieces one between another with a piece of bamboo cane or a long-handled spoon. For exhibition: try to form a design, e.g. layers, contrasting colours, symmetric arrangement.

CONDITION: Such fruit must obviously be clean, disease- and decay-free and there must be no odd pieces of skin, stalk or leaf.

QUANTITY: In such a manner that the topmost pickle is covered by 1cm (½ in) of vinegar and there is a 1cm (½ in) space between the vinegar and the acid-proof cap. An unsuitable cover will let air in to cause serious shrinkage.

FLAVOUR: Have a distinct flavour of the vegetable, fruit or mixture. The spices should not be so strong or unsuitable as to mask the natural flavour. The vinegar must be piquant and not sour, musty, fermented, over-salt or over-sweet.

CLARITY: The vinegar must be brilliantly clear with little or no deposit or cloudiness, usually caused by unsuitable brining or particles of suspended spices.

TEXTURE: Crisp products should be crisp, soft ones should be tender but not squashed or broken. Tough fruits, e.g. damson, may be caused by not pricking through the skins.

A pickle with these qualities may win in an exhibition, but even if it doesn't win it will be a most attractive, nourishing and appetising product, better than those offered in a shop and certainly for much less money.

A SCORE CARD
See page 45 for the maximum number of points awarded for each quality.

For faults, see page 119.

PICKLE VARIETIES

There is a choice of:

1. Raw vegetable (cabbage, cucumber, onion).
2. Raw vegetable (mixed).
3. Cooked vegetable (beetroot, gherkin etc.).
4. Cooked fruit (for all sweet fruits).
5. Piccalilli (covered with a special mixture).

1.   Raw Vegetable Pickle

The operations are:

1. Extract water by placing the vegetable in a brine solution made from 450g (1 lb) salt in 4½ litres (1 gallon) water (or 2 heaped tablespoonfuls per 600ml/1 pint water). Or sprinkle with dry salt to cover.
2. Leave for 24 hours or as specified in the recipes.
3. Drain off the extracted liquid.
4. Pack closely into jars to 2.5cm (1 in) of the top.
5. Pour on cold spiced vinegar to cover 1cm (½ in).
6. Seal airtight.
7. Store cool, dry and dark.

Raw Vegetable Pickle Recipes

Although especially good varieties are given, any vegetables surplus in the garden or available at a cheap rate could certainly be used successfully.

The months given are those when the vegetables are in the best condition and reasonable in price.

CABBAGE (RED)
Select hard and deep-coloured heads. Wash, shred and cover with dry salt for 24 hours. Drain, rinse off the salt, pack fairly tightly, pour in cold spiced vinegar and seal airtight. Can be

used after 14 days but goes limp after 10–12 weeks.

Best variety: Red Drumhead (August–December.)

CABBAGE (WHITE)

Choose *hard* heads. Wash, cut and shred. Dry salt for 24 hours, drain and rinse, pack tightly, fill with cold spiced vinegar and seal airtight. This is a cheap recipe. It can be used after 1 week but loses its crispness in 8 weeks. (August–November.)

CAULIFLOWER

Break the selected heads of white close-knit florets into 1cm (½ in) pieces, brine for 24 hours, drain, rinse, pack, fill with cold vinegar and seal.

Best varieties: Waleseren, Winter Thanet, Andes, Elby F1 Hybrid. (All the year round.)

CUCUMBER (GHERKIN)

Follow the standard recipe. Cut into small pieces, brine for 24 hours, pack in a layer or circle or upright (cut in sticks). Can be used in a week. (July–September.)

NASTURTIUM

Select fully green seeds when dry – but do *not* use the seeds of the Spurge (Euphorbia) which are poisonous. Wash, brine, drain, pack and seal. (September.)

ONION

Choose small hard-fleshed globular onions. Before peeling brine for 12 hours. Then peel, brine afresh for 24 hours, drain, rinse, pot and seal. It is best to wait until the vinegar penetrates through the onion – about 8–10 weeks.

Variety: Paris Silverskin.

A unique pickle is made by grating the onions, salting, draining, washing, potting and covering with white vinegar made pink with cochineal.

SHALLOT

Choose the smaller ones. Follow the *Onion* recipe. Good sorts are Dutch Yellow, Giant Yellow and Atlantic. (July and August.)

WALNUT

Only immature nuts, whose shells have not started to develop, should be used. The shells start to grow at the end opposite the stalk. When the outer skin is pricked with a thin skewer, fork, or large needle, any shell can be felt, and such nuts should not be used.

Brine for 5 days, pour off, brine for 7 days with fresh brine, drain, lay out on dishes until they turn black (about 24–36 hours), pot, add spiced vinegar and seal. It will be ready for use in 6 weeks. Use rubber gloves as the brown stain is not easy to remove. (June and July.)

2.   Mixed Raw Vegetable Pickle

These are a mixture of vegetables selected to balance each other or to improve or complement one another. For example, a vegetable which has a pronounced flavour, like onion, is mixed with a vegetable which has a delicate flavour, like asparagus.

The method used is the same as that for *Raw Vegetable Pickle* on page 98.

Mixed Raw Vegetable Pickle Recipes

ONION, CAULIFLOWER AND CUCUMBER

Peel the onions, break open the cauliflower and cube the cucumber. Mix them together and dry salt for 24 hours. Drain, pack, pour in cold spiced vinegar and seal.

This is the popular 'trade' mixture. For show purposes, pack the vegetables in an attractive pattern (rows and circles), and place 2 whole red chillies (1 each side) into a 300ml (½ pint) jar.

CAULIFLOWER, DWARF BEAN, MARROW AND ONIONS

This is an economical mixture to make use of dwarf or runner beans, late marrow and autumn cauliflower. The quantity of onions used will depend upon personal preferences.

Prepare by slicing the beans moderately thick, and cutting the marrow (or pumpkin) into 1½cm (¾ in) cubes. Brine for 24 hours; brine the marrow separately in dry salt.

Follow the standard recipe as used for *Red Cabbage* (page 98), packing firmly.

ONIONS AND APPLES

An economy mixed pickle made with non-keeping small onions and fallen apples.

Peel the onions, cube or slice the apples and place them at once into salted water for 3 minutes to stop them going brown.

Rather than salting, a preferred method is to use 1 level tablespoonful of salt to 1.15 litres (2 pints) vinegar to cover. It will be ready for use in 7–10 days.

ONIONS AND CUCUMBER

Another economy pickle for surplus produce. Slice the onions, peel and slice or cube the cucumber, dry salt for 24 hours, drain, rinse, pack, fill with spiced vinegar and seal.

Any variety of vegetable can be used to provide an alternative mixture.

3. Cooked Vegetable Pickle

The vegetables used are those which are normally cooked, such as beetroot, carrot, celery, gherkin, mushroom, parsnip, tomato, and they make a most attractive pickle, e.g. orange carrots in white vinegar, macédoine of mixed cubes and slices of carrot, parsnip, turnip, beetroot – most pleasing to the eye and palatable to the taste.

Cooked *root* vegetable pickles are made following the same procedure as used for *Raw Vegetable Pickle* except that:

(a) There is no separate brining;
(b) The vegetables are cooked in slightly salted water (1 tablespoonful salt to 600ml/1 pint water) until firm-tender;
(c) They are covered with *hot* spiced vinegar.

Cooked Vegetable Pickle Recipes

BEETROOT

Wash and place in boiling salted water for 1–1¼ hours without breaking the skins. When still slightly warm, push off the skins, and cut the beetroot into ½cm (¼ in) slices.

Pack carefully into jars, pour on hot spiced vinegar and seal airtight. Use at once.

If it is intended to preserve it for some months, then it should be packed into 450g (1 lb) bottling jars and filled up with boiling-hot spiced vinegar and sealed down with a glass cap and screw band.

Good varieties are Globe, Boltardy Globe, Rubidus F1 Hybrid Globe.

GHERKIN

(Immature cucumber, small ridge cucumber or 'pickling' gherkin.)

Choose those no more than 8cm (3 in) long. Do not peel. Brine for 3 days. Drain, pack into jars, pour in hot spiced vinegar, cover lightly and leave for 24 hours in a warm kitchen.

Drain off the vinegar, bring up to boiling, pour back into the packed jars, cover and leave for another 24 hours. This should result in the gherkins changing to a bright green, though it may be necessary to repeat for a third time if they have not changed colour. After which, make up what hot vinegar is necessary, tidy up the packed vegetables, fill with hot vinegar, and seal airtight.

Good varieties are Venlo Pickling, Bush Champion, Crispy Salad F1 Hybrid (August–September.)

MUSHROOM

Peel, no brining, cook in a casserole dish with *spiced* vinegar to cover until shrunk, pack in layers, cover with the same vinegar hot and seal airtight.

SAMPHIRE

This is a green succulent plant growing on the mud flats of the sea coast. It is delicious and can either be collected or purchased infrequently from the fishmonger or greengrocer.

It is best gathered young in late July and broken into 5cm (2 in) pieces and dry salted for 24 hours. It is then drained and cooked in plain vinegar to cover for a limited period so as not to soften or break down the pieces. Then it is packed horizontally round the jar and covered with plain (not spiced) hot white vinegar. (July–August.)

TOMATO (RIPE)

Red or yellow. Scald and take off the skins of small fruit. No brining. Cover with vinegar as for green tomatoes and cook in an oven (350°F/180°C/gas 4) for half an hour or simmer on the hob for 15–20 minutes. Pack carefully to keep the fruits whole and cover with hot onion vinegar.

Good varieties are: Gardeners Delight, Alicante, Subarctic Plenty.

TOMATO (GREEN)
Slice if firm or halve if soft. Dry salt overnight, drain, cover with vinegar plus one sliced onion and 1 tablespoonful of brown sugar to each 600ml (1 pint), cook firm tender, pack in layers, and fill up with the same hot vinegar. Seal airtight. (October onwards.)

MIXED
Any of the root or special vegetables described above can be mixed and prepared as for the standard recipe.

4. Sweet Fruit Pickle (Spiced Fruit Pickle)

These are a luxury and especially useful for serving with hot or cold meats and all cheeses. They are not brined and are preserved in sweet or plain spiced (special) vinegar.

Suitable fruits are apple (including crab apple), apricot, blackberry, cherry, currant (black), damson, gooseberry, grape, peach, pear, plum and rhubarb.

Here is the method:

1. Select, wash and prepare sound, firm, ripe fruit; whole fruits should be pricked to avoid shrivelling.
2. Dissolve 1kg (2 lb) sugar to 1.8kg (4 lb) fruit in 600ml (1 pint) water (except for special recipes given later).
3. Add the recommended spices (tied in a muslin bag) – see below.
4. Put all in a saucepan and simmer gently (keeping the saucepan lid on) until firm-tender but not soft.
5. Drain off the vinegar carefully.
6. Pack the fruit into jars to within ½–2½cm (¼–1 in) of the top.
7. Boil the vinegar-syrup (with the saucepan lid off) until it is 'syrupy'.
8. Pour the hot vinegar onto the packed fruit to cover 1cm (½ in).
9. Seal airtight without delay
10. Store dark, dry and cool.
11. Try to keep them for 6–8 weeks before using.

N.B. The spices must be suitable for fruits, i.e. aromatic spices, and not those used for vegetable pickle.

Suitable *aromatic* spice mixtures are:

MINISTRY OF AGRICULTURE SPICE MIXTURE
15g (½ oz) whole cloves
7g (¼ oz) root ginger
9g (⅓ oz) pimento (allspice)
7g (¼ oz) stick cinnamon
Rind of ½ lemon

'GRANGE' SPICE MIXTURE
7g (¼ oz) mace
7g (¼ oz) cinnamon
100g (4 oz) pimento (allspice)
100g (4 oz) cloves
7g (¼ oz) ginger root
7g (¼ oz) coriander

The above quantities are for use with 1.15 litres (2 pints) vinegar, 1.8kg (4 lb) sugar and 3½kg (8 lb) stone fruit or pears. Half the above quantities are used with 600ml (1 pint) vinegar, 1kg (2 lb) sugar and 1.8kg (4 lb) fruit.

Sweet Fruit Pickle (Spiced Fruit Pickle) Recipes

APPLE
2kg (4½ lb) apples (peeled, cored and sliced), 1.8kg (4 lb) sugar, 1.15 litres (2 pints) spiced vinegar. Simmer all in a saucepan until tender. Drain, pack in a jar. Boil the hot vinegar to a syrup, pour onto the fruit to 1cm (½ in), seal airtight.

CRAB APPLE
Cook 1.4kg (3 lb) crab apples (whole and unskinned) until firm-tender with ¼ lemon and its peel in enough water to cover the fruit.

Put 600ml (1 pint) malt vinegar (for flavour), 1kg (2 lb) sugar and 300ml (½ pint) of the fruit cooking water, along with a muslin bag of spices, into a saucepan to boil. Add the cooked crab apples and simmer gently until the syrup has become 'adhesive' (about 30–35 minutes). Pack the fruit into hot jars, pour on the hot syrup and seal.

A good spice mixture is 5cm (2 in) cinnamon stick, 2 pieces of ginger root and 2 cloves.

APRICOT

2kg (4½ lb) apricots, 1.4kg (3 lb) white sugar, 1.15 litres (2 pints) white vinegar to enhance the colour.

Halve and stone the apricots. Cook them gently on top of the cooker until the skins peel. Dissolve the sugar in the vinegar, add spices and boil in a saucepan until syrupy. Pack the apricots into jars and pour on the thick hot spiced vinegar and seal.

BLACKBERRY OR BLACK CURRANT

1.8kg (4 lb) fruit, 1kg (2 lb) sugar, 600ml (1 pint) white unspiced vinegar, 15g (½ oz) cloves, 15g (½ oz) pimento (allspice), 15g (½ oz) cinnamon. Follow the standard method.

CHERRY

1.8kg (4 lb) cherries (the best sorts being Morello, May Duke and Kentish Red), 1kg (2 lb) sugar, 600ml (1 pint) *unspiced* white vinegar, 4 cloves, 15g (½ oz) root ginger. Follow the standard method.

CUCUMBER (SWEET)

1.4kg (3 lb) cucumber, 1kg (2 lb) sugar, 600ml (1 pint) spiced vinegar. Cut the cucumber into convenient shapes. Cover in plain cold vinegar for 4 days, then follow the standard method.

DAMSON

1.8kg (4 lb) fruit, 1kg (2 lb) sugar, ¼ lemon and its peel, 600ml (1 pint) spiced white vinegar. Follow the standard method.

GOOSEBERRY

2¼kg (5 lb) fruit, 1.4kg (3 lb) sugar, 1.15 litres (2 pints) spiced vinegar. Use green gooseberries and simmer carefully to avoid squashing. Follow the standard method.

GRAPE (SMALL OUTDOOR)

1.8kg (4 lb) fruit, 1kg (2 lb) sugar, 600ml (1 pint) white spiced vinegar. It is best to cook the grapes in a slow oven first and then to pack and cover with hot spiced white vinegar.

PEACH (FRESH)

Follow the *Apricot* recipe. Skin with boiling water, blanch and halve.

PEAR

1.8kg (4 lb) fruit, 1kg (2 lb) sugar, 600ml (1 pint) spiced vinegar (brown malt for flavour, ¼ lemon and peel). Follow the standard method. This is excellent with pork.

PLUM

It is best to choose small firm-ripe 'cooking' plums.

1.8kg (4 lb) fruit, 1kg (2 lb) sugar, 600ml (1 pint) spiced vinegar, ¼ lemon and its peel. Remove the plum stones and follow the standard method.

RHUBARB

1.4kg (3 lb) fruit, 1kg (2 lb) sugar, 600ml (1 pint) spiced vinegar. Cut the rhubarb into 2½cm (1 in) pieces and follow the standard method.

5. Piccalilli

This is a mixture of vegetables in a thick yellow sauce which can be pungent, sour, sweet, hot or mild. It is most useful, appetite-rousing and popular. Any vegetables, which are surplus or cheap, can be used, even ones that are deformed or diseased, so long as only the wholesome parts are selected.

The most suitable vegetables are: beans (dwarf, runner and broad), cabbage (white or red), capsicum, cauliflower, celery, cucumber, gherkin, marrow, nasturtium seed, onion, shallot and tomato.

To prepare the vegetables remove any diseased or decayed parts, clean, peel, divide and cut them up into small even pieces.

INGREDIENTS FOR A 'HOT' PICCALILLI:

30g (1¼ oz) ground ginger
30g (1¼ oz) dry mustard
15g (½ oz) turmeric
20g (¾ oz) cornflour or flour
175g (6 oz) white sugar
1.15 litres (2 pints) white vinegar

INGREDIENTS FOR A 'SWEET' PICCALILLI:

7g (¼ oz) ground ginger
15g (½ oz) dry mustard
7g (¼ oz) turmeric

25g (1 oz) cornflour or flour
225g (8 oz) white sugar
1.4 litres (2½ pints) white vinegar

Here is the method:

1. Prepare 2¾kg (6 lb) vegetables.
2. Place them in a wide, shallow dish and sprinkle with dry salt, layer by layer, and leave for 24 hours to draw out the water.
3. Drain, rinse and place in a cooking vessel, together with the required quantity of white vinegar, spices, sugar and turmeric, depending on whether a hot or sweet piccalilli is required (see above), putting aside 150ml (¼ pint) of the vinegar for use later. Simmer until the vegetables are either crisp or soft as desired, but not over-cooked or squashy.
4. Blend the cornflour or flour with the reserved vinegar and stir this into the cooked vegetables.
5. Bring to the boil, stirring occasionally and boil for 3 minutes.
6. Pour into hot jars, taking care to have an even distribution of vegetables in each jar.
7. Seal airtight.

An alternative is to strain off the vinegar from the vegetables after cooking, pack into the jars *and then* pour on the thick sauce to cover.

7

CHUTNEYS, SAUCES
AND KETCHUPS

CHUTNEYS

A CHUTNEY is a mixture of fruits and/or vegetables (fresh or dried), cooked with sugar, spices and vinegar. It is a most rewarding preserve, quick and easy to make, uses cheap or low-quality or glut produce and is a valuable supplement to many meat or fish dishes.

The most popular basic fruits are: apple, blackberry, damson, elderberry, gooseberry, plum, rhubarb and tomatoes (green or red). The most useful vegetables are: beetroot and marrow.

These are the *basic* ingredients. To these are added products for their flavour, e.g. salt, spice, raisins, dates, onion, ginger, and sugar (demerara and brown) and vinegar (brown malt for flavour, white for light-coloured produce) all cooked together long and slow to produce this economical and satisfying mixture. Vegetables which are rather tough may be cooked tender first in some of the vinegar and spices.

Equipment

The *cooking pan* can be of stainless steel, uncracked enamel, glass and aluminium, but *not* of iron, brass or copper, which is acted upon to cause an unpleasant taste and peculiar colour.

Sieves should not be of metal other than stainless steel, but of hair, nylon or an acceptable plastic.

Jars. It is most important that chutneys are capped so that they will always remain tight. Many chutneys improve with keeping but if air gets in, they sink down in the jar, become hard and unappetising.

A screw-capped jar with cork, ceresin or plastic lining is the only satisfactory cover.

The Standard Recipe

The simple operation is:

1. Select and prepare the fruits and/or vegetables.
2. Chop or mince fine. (This is considered the best way but some people may prefer a coarse chutney with medium or large pieces).
3. Place in a pan with whole spices in a muslin bag or ground spices (usually preferred), plus the other ingredients as per the recipe, e.g. onion, raisins, dates (not sugar), and just cover with vinegar.
4. Put the lid on the pan and simmer gently until all the ingredients are soft. The secret is slow and long cooking, perhaps for 1–4 hours.
5. Dissolve the sugar in the remaining vinegar and add to the cooked lot.
6. Cook gently (with the lid off the pan), stir frequently until the consistency is that of jam (remembering that chutney when it cools becomes thicker than when it was hot).
7. Fill up without delay into hot jars to 1cm (½ in) of the top. Seal airtight.
8. Label and store away in a cool, dark, dry place for at least two months.

What is a Good Chutney?

COVER: Airtight with a cork, ceresin, plastic or some vinegar-lining beneath the metal cap.

LABEL AND DATE: Most helpful (especially as a chutney should be at least two months old before use) but often omitted. Note on the label the date, the variety and other useful brief details.

CLEANLINESS: No dirt or rust on caps, no smears on glass inside or outside.

PACKING: To within 1cm (½ in) of the cap. Stored warm and with an air-loose cover, a chutney will lose one-third of its volume in ten weeks and become dry and unpleasant.

COLOUR: The more brilliant, the more attractive. Make use of the natural fruit or vegetable colour and show an even colour all through.

PREPARATION: Careful mincing and chopping, etc.

TEXTURE: Soft, mellow and even, with all produce blended. Skins should be soft and there should be no hard particles. On the other hand, where a chutney is preferred in which the pieces are easily distinguished, so well and good!

FLAVOUR: Distinct, pleasing, lively, balanced, appetite-boosting which enhances a cold meal. Much depends on one's own tastes. Must never be mouldy, musty, sour, bitter, fermented or excessively hot or sweet.

A SCORE CARD
See page 45 for the maximum number of points awarded for each quality.

For faults, see page 119.

Special Recipes

These can always be adjusted to be hot, mild, sweet or sharp by varying the amount of spice, sugar, etc. Hot chutneys require 1.8kg (4 lb) fruit, 1 teaspoonful each of mustard and ground ginger and ½ teaspoonful cayenne pepper and 7g (¼ oz) curry powder.

Level spoonfuls are used.

Sultanas can be replaced by raisins, currants or dates. Onions can be partly or wholly replaced with shallots. Be very wary if you use garlic – even with a few cloves. Dried fruit can be used in place of fresh fruit when a quarter of the sugar can be omitted. Colourful fruits demand white sugar and white vinegar.

The consistency can be varied at the final cooking: if you want it thicker, cook it for longer; if it is too thick, add 150ml (¼ pint) vinegar.

APPLE
2¾kg (6 lb) apples, 450g (1 lb) onions, 450g (1 lb) sultanas, 28g (1 oz) salt, 1.4kg (3 lb) sugar, 1¾ litres (3 pints) vinegar, 28g

(1 oz) ground ginger, ¾ teaspoonful cayenne. Yield: 4½–5kg (10–11 lb).

BEETROOT
1.8kg (4 lb) cooked beetroot, 225g (½ lb) onions, 450g (1 lb) raisins (or sultanas), 15g (½ oz) salt, 225g (½ lb) white sugar, 600ml (1 pint) white vinegar, 6 peppercorns, 6 cloves, 1 tablespoonful pimento (allspice).

BLACKBERRY
2¾kg (6 lb) blackberries, 675g (1½ lb) apples, 1kg (2 lb) onions, 75g (3 oz) salt, 1kg (2 lb) brown sugar, 1.15 litres (2 pints) brown malt vinegar, 50g (2 oz) ground ginger, 1 teaspoonful cayenne, 2 tablespoonfuls mustard, 1½ teaspoonfuls powdered mace. Pips should be removed by passing the cooked blackberries through a sieve. Yield: 3½–4kg (8–9 lb).

DAMSON
1.4kg (3 lb) damsons, 675g (1½ lb) apples, 450g (1 lb) onions, 450g (1 lb) sultanas, 38g (1½ oz) salt, 225g (½ lb) white sugar, 1.15 litres (2 pints) white vinegar, 1 teaspoonful pimento (allspice), ½ teaspoonful mustard (can be omitted), 1 teaspoonful ground ginger, ¼ teaspoonful each of cayenne and mace. Remove the stones. Yield: 2¼kg (5 lb).

ELDERBERRY
1.4kg (3 lb) elderberries, 225g (½ lb) onions, 1.8kg (4 lb) sultanas, 28g (1 oz) salt, 225g (½ lb) sugar, 600ml (1 pint) vinegar, 1 teaspoonful each of pimento (allspice), cinnamon, cayenne and ground ginger. Use berries which are just ripe, not over-ripe. Yield: 1.6–1.8kg (3½–4 lb).

GOOSEBERRY
1.4kg (3 lb) gooseberries, 225g (½ lb) onions, 225g (½ lb) sultanas, 20g (¾ oz) salt, 450g (1 lb) sugar, 900ml (1½ pints) vinegar, 1 tablespoonful each of pimento (allspice) and ground ginger, ¼ teaspoonful cayenne. Half the vinegar can be tarragon vinegar. Yield: 1.8–2kg (4–4½ lb).

MARROW
1.8kg (4 lb) marrow, 675g (1½ lb) apples, 450g (1 lb) onions, 50g (2 oz) salt, 450g (1 lb) sugar, 1.8kg (4 lb) sultanas, 1¾ litres (3 pints) vinegar, 2 tablespoonfuls each of peppercorns,

mustard seed and cut up ginger root. Yield: about 3kg (6½–7 lb).

PLUM

1.8kg (4 lb) plums. Follow the *Damson* recipe but use 25g (1 oz) salt and 225g (½ lb) chopped stoned raisins in place of the sultanas. Yield: 2–2¼kg (4½–5 lb).

RHUBARB

1.8kg (4 lb) rhubarb, 450g (1 lb) onions, 450g (1 lb) sultanas or raisins, 15g (½ oz) salt, 675g (1½ lb) sugar, 900ml (1½ pints) vinegar, 450g (1 lb) apples (optional), 1 tablespoonful each of ground ginger and pimento (allspice) and, if desired, of curry powder. Yield: 2¼–2¾kg (5–6 lb).

TOMATO (GREEN)

1.8kg (4 lb) tomatoes, 450g (1 lb) apples, 350g (¾ lb) onions, 350g (¾ lb) sultanas, 15g (½ oz) salt, 450g (1 lb) brown sugar, 700ml (1¼ pints) vinegar, 1 tablespoonful each of mustard seed and root ginger (in a muslin bag) and ¼ teaspoonful cayenne. One dessertspoonful curry powder can be added if desired. Yield: 2¾–3¼kg (6–7 lb).

TOMATO (RED)

1.8kg (4 lb) tomatoes, 100g (4 oz) onions, 15g (½ oz) salt, 225g (½ lb) white sugar, 300ml (½ pint) white vinegar, 1 teaspoonful each of cayenne, cloves and ginger (or mace). Yield: 1.6–1.8kg (3½–4 lb).

INDIAN CHUTNEY

1.8kg (4 lb) apples, 100g (4 oz) onions, 1kg (2 lb) sultanas, 20g (¾ oz) salt, 1¼kg (2½ lb) soft brown sugar, 1.15 litres (2 pints) brown malt vinegar, 50g (2 oz) ground ginger, 1 teaspoonful cayenne, 25g (1 oz) ground mustard.

SAUCES

A sauce is a semi-liquid chutney that is made from the same type of ingredients but after the preliminary cooking (and before adding the sugar, salt and part vinegar), the mass is sieved so as to produce a smooth purée which when prepared further will result in a delicious and wholesome sauce of great value in the kitchen.

The most suitable fruits are apple, blackberry, red currant, damson, elderberry, plum, rhubarb and tomato.

Equipment

As well as the usual equipment required for making chutney, a *sterilizer* is needed for some sauces, e.g. tomato sauce. Any deep pan can be used for this purpose. A trivet, wooden base or folded newspaper is placed on the base to prevent the bottles from cracking. See Fig. 9. You will need *oven gloves* to remove the bottles from the pan once some of the water has been ladled or tipped out.

Fig. 9. Sterilizing.
A good home-made sterilizer is a vessel deep enough to allow for covering the bottles to the caps with water, and has a false bottom of a piece of wood, a trivet or folded newspaper to stop the bottles cracking at the bottom.

The Standard Method

1. Select the fruit, prepare by cutting it into small pieces, cubes or slices.
2. Cook to soften thoroughly.
3. Strain through a hair sieve or muslin.
4. Place in a pan and add the sugar, salt, vinegar and spices (in a muslin bag) or use spiced vinegar.
5. Cook gently until the mixture is of the consistency of thick cream (remembering that it will get thicker when cold). It must be free to pour out of the bottle.
6. For those sauces which do not need to be sterilized, pour the sauce into warm bottles without delay and seal airtight. Bottles with corks sealed with paraffin wax or with ceresin-lined screw tops may be used.
7. For those sauces which need to be sterilized (see individual recipes), pour the sauce into warm bottles and heat them, with loose caps, in a water bath for the necessary time, and then screw down each jar at once.
8. Store in a dry, cool, dark place.

What is a Good Sauce?

COVER: Airtight, clean and with a vinegar-proof lining.

COLOUR: Bright, not dull, cloudy or streaky.

TEXTURE: Even and smooth all through with no pips, peel, skins or lumps. No free liquid.

CONSISTENCY: As a sauce semi-soft: to pour slowly without undue shaking, but not to run out in a thin stream.

FLAVOUR: Most important. Preferably neither over-hot, sweet or salty: no mould, mustiness, bitterness, neither sharp nor irritant.

A SCORE CARD

The score card of points is similar to that for chutneys (see page 45).

For faults, see page 119.

Special Recipes

APPLE

1kg (2 lb) apples, 3½ teaspoonfuls sugar, 300ml (½ pint) water (preferably soft), 25g (1 oz) butter.

Cut the apples finely, put all in a saucepan and simmer until the mixture is soft. To improve smoothness, the apples should be beaten or pressed. This will keep safely if put into warm jars and sterilized at 82°C (180°F) for half an hour, and then the caps screwed down to seal, or corks sterilized, pushed well in and sealed with paraffin wax.

BLACKBERRY

1.8kg (4 lb) blackberries, 450g (1 lb) apples, 225g (½ lb) onions, 50g (2 oz) salt, 450–675g (1–1½ lb) sugar, 1.15 litres (2 pints) vinegar, 1 level teaspoonful each of cinnamon, pimento (allspice), ground ginger and mace.

DAMSON

1.8kg (4 lb) damsons, 225g (½ lb) onions, 100g (4 oz) raisins, 35g (1¼ oz) salt, 225g (½ lb) white sugar, 900ml (1½ pints) white vinegar, 7g (¼ oz) each of ground ginger, pimento (allspice) and mace, and 2 level teaspoonfuls each of peppercorns and chillies (and 1 teaspoonful mustard if desired).

Cut up the damsons, remove the stones, slice the onions, stone the raisins, add the spices and 450ml (¾ pint) vinegar and cook slowly until soft (25–35 minutes). Sieve the pulp, add the salt, sugar and 450ml (¾ pint) vinegar and cook very slowly until creamy (50–65 minutes). Bottle hot and cover at once.

ELDERBERRY

1.8kg (4 lb) elderberries, 100g (4 oz) onions, 35g (1¼ oz) salt, 450g–1kg (1–2 lb) sugar (according to preference), 600ml (1 pint) vinegar, 1 level teaspoonful each of cinnamon, pimento (allspice), ground ginger and cayenne. This is excellent with fish.

PLUM

Follow the *Damson* recipe, using currants in place of the raisins. Use blue plums if possible.

RHUBARB

1.8kg (4 lb) rhubarb, 1.4kg (3 lb) onions, 20g (¾ oz) salt, 1kg

(2 lb) sugar, 1.15 litres (2 pints) brown malt vinegar (for flavour), 1 teaspoonful each of peppercorns, chillies, ginger, pimento (allspice) and, if you like, curry powder.

Cut up the rhubarb and onions, cook all together, except for the sugar, for 1¼–2¼ hours. Sieve, add the sugar and cook again until medium-thick. This is a well-flavoured and cheap sauce.

TOMATO
Tomato sauces are not usually good keepers and so they should be sterilized at 82°C (180°F) for 30 minutes and then sealed airtight with the screw caps or corks secured in place (special bottles can be purchased).

TOMATO (RED)
1.8kg (4 lb) tomatoes, 225g (½ lb) onions (if desired), 15g (½ oz) salt, 225g (½ lb) sugar, 675g (1½ lb) apples (if desired), 300ml (½ pint) white vinegar, 1 level teaspoonful each of cloves, ginger and mace. Sterilize as above. A popular sauce for use at any time.

TOMATO (YELLOW, RIPE)
These tomatoes make a unique sauce following the above recipe with the apples but not the onions.

TOMATO (GREEN, UNRIPE)
1.8kg (4 lb) tomatoes, 675g (1½ lb) apples, 100g (4 oz) onions, 25g (1 oz) salt, 450g (1 lb) sugar, 600ml (1 pint) vinegar, 1 dessertspoonful celery seed (if desired) and 1 teaspoonful each of mustard seed, peppercorns and root ginger (in a muslin bag). This sauce has an excellent flavour and is a good way to use up the end-of-season unripe tomatoes.

HORSERADISH SAUCE
This is a special recipe:

1. Scrape, grate or mince plump, juicy horseradish root.
2. Without delay, place in a boiling solution of brine (1 level teaspoonful salt to 600ml/1 pint water) for one minute.
3. Drain and pack in jars.
4. Cover at once with boiling white vinegar.
5. Seal airtight.

It is better not to add cream until the sauce is to be used: 1 teacup of cream and 1 level teaspoonful sugar is mixed in with each heaped dessertspoonful of horseradish (in vinegar).

KETCHUPS

A KETCHUP is a thin 'sauce' which pours readily from a bottle, the thicker parts of the pulp having been sieved out. If the consistency of a ketchup is preferred to the thicker texture of a sauce, then the sauce recipes, as given here, can be adjusted so that (a) the fine portions are strained out for the ketchup, and (b) the thicker part used as a chutney.

The ideal ketchup is a thin, bright, flavoursome product of extreme value for cold and hot meals, game and fish.

Sterilizing

As many of these ketchups are likely to ferment in store (especially those with little acid such as tomato, mushroom and walnut), it is a safeguard to sterilize them by heating them with loose caps in a water-bath for 15 minutes at 82°C/180°F (simmering) and then screwing down each jar at once. It is possible to seal after sterilization with corks and paraffin wax (see stage 6, page 114).

Spiced Vinegars

The recipes for these are given on page 95. The spices may vary according to taste, but they should not be so profuse that the flavour of the fruit is masked.

The most popular ketchups are those made from apple, blackberry, damson, elderberry, gooseberry, mushroom, tomato and walnut.

Recipes

APPLE

1.8kg (4 lb) apples, 225g (½ lb) onions, 25g (1 oz) salt, 225g (½ lb) sugar, 600ml (1 pint) spiced vinegar.

An easy method is to chop the apples and onions finely, place them in a pan with the salt and spiced vinegar and cook long and gentle until the pulp is in a finely mashed state.

Pass this through a fine hair sieve, add the sugar, stir well in and boil for 5 minutes. Fill hot into hot bottles and sterilize.

BLACKBERRY

1.8kg (4 lb) blackberries, 7g (¼ oz) salt, 225g (½ lb) sugar, 900ml (1½ pints) spiced vinegar.

Just cover the blackberries with water and simmer until well cooked. Pass through a fine sieve to exclude the pips. Add this to the salt (if desired), sugar and spiced vinegar and boil for 5 minutes. Bottle hot and sterilize.

DAMSON

1.8kg (4 lb) damsons, 450g (1 lb) sugar, 700ml (1¼ pints) spiced vinegar, 7g (¼ oz) salt.

Simmer the fruit, sugar and spiced vinegar together in a covered pan until all the pulp has disintegrated and the maximum liquid has been produced. Strain (i.e. sieve the ketchup, pressing the pulp to extract all the liquid from the damsons), add the salt and boil gently for 5 minutes. Bottle hot and sterilize.

ELDERBERRY

1.8kg (4 lb) elderberries, 7g (¼ oz) salt, 225g (½ lb) onions, 900ml (1½ pints) spiced vinegar, (225g/½ lb sugar if a sweeter ketchup is preferred).

Simmer the fruit with the vinegar until all the juice has been extracted, strain, add the salt and onions and boil for 4–5 minutes. Take out the onions, bottle, cap hot and sterilize.

GOOSEBERRY

1.8kg (4 lb) gooseberries, 1kg (2 lb) sugar, 600ml (1 pint) spiced malt vinegar. Cook all together for an hour, strain and bottle hot.

MUSHROOM (Very popular.)

1.8kg (4 lb) mushrooms, 100–125g (4–5 oz) salt, one small onion (chopped fine), 600ml (1 pint) spiced vinegar.

Skin and mince the mushrooms and stalk, sprinkle with salt and leave for 2–3 days, stirring frequently.

Place all the ingredients and liquor in a pan and cook gently for 1½–2 hours. Strain, bottle and sterilize.

TOMATO (Most popular.)

1.8kg (4 lb) tomatoes, 100g (4 oz) onions, 15g (½ oz) salt, 175g (6 oz) sugar, 225g (½ lb) apples, 450ml (¾ pint) spiced vinegar.

Slice the tomatoes, onions and apples, and simmer together, stirring frequently to avoid burning, until all the pulp has disintegrated and the maximum liquid has been produced. Strain, add to the sugar, salt and spiced vinegar, and boil carefully for 5 minutes, bottle hot and sterilize.

WALNUT (Another popular one.)

Cut in half and crush 70 soft green walnuts as used for pickling. Place in a jar with 175g (6 oz) chopped onions or shallots, 175g (6 oz) salt and 1¾ litres (3 pints) boiling spiced vinegar. Stir well to dissolve the salt, mix all well together and allow to stand for 5 days, stirring each day.

Then pour the liquid part through a fine strainer, simmer for 1 hour, bottle and sterilize.

PICKLING, CHUTNEY AND SAUCE FAULTS

CLOUDY LIQUID

Use of poor quality vinegar, low in acid; failure to cook (as per recipe); early deterioration through lack of proper procedure, e.g. short brining period or use of a low salt brine; presence of ground spices probably of poor quality.

SHRINKAGE IN JAR

Evaporation in warm store; loose cover or use of one which is not airtight; careless packing so that vegetables sink down and leave spaces.

LOOSE VINEGAR

Often occurs with chutneys and sauces which have not followed a satisfactory recipe or which have not been cooked for a sufficient length of time to ensure complete integration.

TOUGH FRUITS

E.g. damsons and plums. Fruit should be pricked to allow vinegar to permeate right through. Fruits are hard and almost 'raw'.

COLOUR CHANGE

In chutneys and sauces, there may be a ½–1cm (¼–½ in) layer which is of darker colour than that beneath. This may be due to air contamination, to short cooking, warm or long storage.

BAD COLOUR

Especially in tomato sauce is usually due to darkening through the use of brown sugar and brown malt vinegar or to some over-cooking after sugar is added.

USEFUL HINTS

Oven temperatures (approximate)

Extremely hot	475°F/245°C/gas 9
Very hot	450°F/230°C/gas 8
Hot	430°F/220°C/gas 7
Moderately hot	400°F/205°C/gas 6
Moderately warm	370°F/190°C/gas 5
Moderate	350°F/180°C/gas 4
Very moderate	340°F/170°C/gas 3
Slow	300°F/150°C/gas 2
Cool	280°F/140°C/gas 1
Very slow	250°F/120°C/gas ½
Very cool	240°F/115°C/gas ¼

To convert Fahrenheit to Centigrade: take away 32, multiply by 5 and divide by 9.

To convert Centigrade to Fahrenheit: multiply by 9, divide by 5 and add 32.

For example:

$$32°F = 0°C$$
$$65°F = 18°C$$
$$104°F = 40°C$$
$$122°F = 50°C$$
$$140°F = 60°C$$
$$158°F = 70°C$$
$$176°F = 80°C$$
$$194°F = 90°C$$
$$212°F = 100°C$$

Water boils at 100°C (212°F).
Jam usually sets at 104–105°C (220–222°F).

Jelly usually sets at 104–105°C (220–221°F).

Fruit (etc.) is sterilized at 74–80°C (165–175°F) *except* for cherries, pears, and tomatoes which are sterilized at 82–87°C (180–190°F).

Vegetables are sterilized at 4.5kg (10 lb) pressure (115°C/240°F).

Syrup is sterilized at 77°C (170°F).

Light syrup: 100g (4 oz) sugar to 600ml (1 pint).
Medium syrup: 225–275g (8–10 oz) sugar to 600ml (1 pint).
Heavy syrup: 350–450g (12–16 oz) sugar to 600ml (1 pint).

Pressure Cooker Temperatures

Pressures:	Temperature:
2.25kg (5 lb)	108°C (227°F)
3.5kg (8 lb)	112°C (233°F)
4.5kg (10 lb)	115°C (240°F)
5.8kg (13 lb)	118°C (245°F)
6.8kg (15 lb)	121°C (250°F)

Capacity (approximate)

Remember: when following the recipes, always follow one set of measurements and never mix metric and imperial.

150ml	= ¼ pint (5 fl oz)
300ml	= ½ pint (10 fl oz)
450ml	= ¾ pint (15 fl oz)
600ml	= 1 pint (20 fl oz)
700ml	= 1¼ pints
900ml	= 1½ pints
990ml	= 1¾ pints
1.15 litres	= 2 pints
1.4 litres	= 2½ pints
1.75 litres	= 3 pints
2 litres	= 3½ pints
2.3 litres	= 4 pints
2.5 litres	= 4½ pints
2.8 litres	= 5 pints

3 litres   = 5½ pints
3.5 litres = 6 pints
4.5 litres = 8 pints (1 gallon)
6.8 litres = 12 pints

QUICK MEASURE
1 wineglass = 70ml (2½ fl oz)
1 teacup = 150ml (¼ pint)
1 breakfast cup = 300ml (½ pint)
1 tablespoon = 28ml (1 fl oz)

Weight (approximate)

25g   = 1 oz
50g   = 2 oz
75g   = 3 oz
100g   = 4 oz (¼ lb)
175g   = 6 oz
225g   = 8 oz (½ lb)
350g   = 12 oz (¾ lb)
400g   = 14 oz
450g   = 16 oz (1 lb)
550g   = 1¼ lb
675g   = 1½ lb
1kg   = 2 lb
1.4kg   = 3 lb
1.8kg   = 4 lb
2.25kg = 5 lb
2.75kg = 6 lb
3.25kg = 7 lb
3.5kg   = 8 lb
4kg   = 9 lb
4.5kg   = 10 lb
5kg   = 11 lb
5.5kg   = 12 lb

QUICK KITCHEN WEIGHTS (APPROXIMATE)
The following gives the approximate number of level (not heaped) tablespoons required to make 25g (1 oz) of each ingredient:

Dried Fruit

Currants	2	Sultanas	2
Raisins	2	Peel (cut fine)	1

Powders

Cocoa	3	Coconut	4
Coffee (ground)	4	Coffee (vacuum)	6½
Cornflour	2	Custard	2
Flour	3	Macaroni (flaked)	4
Milk (dried)	4	Rice	2
Rice (flaked)	4	Rice (ground)	3
Sago	2½	Semolina	2
Tapioca	2	Tapioca (flaked)	4

Syrup

Honey (runny)	1	Icing	4
Sugar (most)	2	Sugar (brown)	3
Treacle	1		

INDEX

FREE

If you would like an up-to-date list of all **RIGHT WAY** titles currently available, please send a stamped self-addressed envelope to

ELLIOT RIGHT WAY BOOKS, KINGSWOOD, SURREY, KT20 6TD, U.K.